The Money Intelligence

Mike Feng Zheng

ISBN: 978-1-80128-833-0

Dedication

To my father, Shide Zheng, who taught me to see the world at its full potential.

My mother, BiYun Wang, was always more concerned about her children than herself.

My wife, Ying Chen, for her immense support.

To my daughters, Wendy Zheng and Willa Zheng, I am excited to grow alongside you.

Acknowledgments

The Money Intelligence, like any other book, would not have been written without the assistance of many people who helped me along the way.

There are way too many people to acknowledge for this to be a complete list.

On the other hand, a selected few have been incredibly supportive, including Paul Smith, who assisted me and provided direction throughout the process.

Michelle Young is someone who inspires, directs, and grounds me.

My wife, Ying Chen, and my daughter, Wendy Zheng, are tremendous sources of support and encouragement for me.

About the Author

Mike Feng Zheng is an entrepreneur, financier, and author.

He was born in China and moved to the U.S. in 1996. He is interested in writing books in various genres, such as investment, self-help, and fantasy.

He is the author and co-author of several books, including The Art of Money: An Ultimate Guide to Pursuing Prosperity and Happiness, 12 Principles for Life, Ten More Principles for Life, Skullduggery Nightmares, and Whisper in the Storm.

Mike Feng Zheng is married and has two daughters. His older daughter, Wendy, who is ten years old, is also an author. They are currently residing in Dallas, Texas.

Contents

Introduction - The Supreme Stage of Human Experience

In a bustling city, there lived a renowned heart surgeon, Dr. Wilson, who was famous for his exceptional skills and wealthy lifestyle. He had earned his degree from a prestigious university and was admired by his peers for his professional accomplishments. Despite his success, Dr. Wilson had a complicated relationship with money, often showing off his wealth unnecessarily and foolishly. He would drive his luxury cars recklessly, frequently boasting about how much he had spent on them, and treated his possession as a status symbol to flaunt in front of others.

Dr. Wilson's social life revolved around attending high-end clubs and exclusive events, where he would make extravagant purchases to impress those around him. He was known for picking up the tab for everyone at the bar or buying lavish gifts for his acquaintances. This behavior was driven by his desire to maintain a particular image, even if it meant jeopardizing his financial well-being.

Unfortunately, Dr. Wilson's financial decisions were often impulsive and poorly thought out. His reckless spending and lack of planning for the future eventually caught up with him. As his debts piled up, he found it increasingly difficult to maintain his extravagant lifestyle. He was forced to sell his luxurious home and valuable possessions, which was insufficient to pull him out of his financial hole.

On the other side of town, there lived a woman named Mary. She was a hardworking, middle-aged schoolteacher who had never attended college. Mary came from a modest background and was always careful with her money. She didn't possess a formal education in finance but had an innate sense of frugality and responsibility. Her approach to money was guided by practicality rather than the desire for social status.

Mary lived in a small, well-kept home that she had purchased within her means. She rarely indulged in luxuries, focusing instead on saving and investing her money wisely. Although her salary was a fraction of Dr. Wilson's, her careful planning and financial discipline allowed her to live comfortably and avoid falling into debt.

Over the years, Mary's frugal lifestyle and wise investments slowly but steadily grew her wealth. She could send her children to college, take modest vacations, and still have enough money to retire comfortably. She was well-respected in her community, not for her material possessions, but for her kindness, wisdom, and financial stability.

When Mary passed away, she left a significant sum to her loved ones, ensuring their financial security for years. On the other hand, Dr. Wilson lost everything and struggled to rebuild his life. His once-glamorous existence had crumbled, leaving him with little more than a painful lesson in the consequences of poor financial behavior.

The essence of this tale is that financial success isn't solely determined by intelligence or education. Instead, it often hinges on an individual's behavior and mindset regarding money. A higher level of expertise correlates with tremendous success in many fields. However, when it comes to personal finance, even someone with no formal education can outperform a highly educated individual if they possess the right behavioral skills and mindset.

The world of finance is frequently viewed as a numbers game, where calculations and formulas dictate actions. While this approach isn't inherently flawed, it often overlooks the importance of financial decision-making's emotional and psychological aspects. Recognizing the significance of these "soft skills" and incorporating them into one's financial strategies can lead to tremendous success and security in the long run.

In a quaint town named Serenity, two friends named Amelia and Benjamin grew up together. They attended the same school, played in the same parks, and even worked at the same local grocery store during their teenage years. Their lives followed parallel paths until they left Serenity to pursue higher education.

Amelia studied at a prestigious university and earned a degree in finance, graduating with top honors. She was recruited by a leading investment firm, where she quickly climbed the ranks and became a renowned financial analyst. Her life was filled with wealth, luxury, and prestige. Benjamin, on the other hand, chose a different path. He attended a small community college and studied psychology, focusing on human behavior and emotions. Upon graduating, he returned to Serenity and became a high school guidance counselor, helping students navigate their emotional and academic challenges.

As the years went by, Amelia's career flourished. She was featured in industry magazines and gave keynote speeches at financial conferences. However, her personal life suffered as she often made impulsive financial decisions driven by the latest trends and the fear of missing out. She accumulated debt, failed to save for the future, and became increasingly stressed about her financial situation. Her wealth and professional success did not bring her the happiness she had hoped for.

Benjamin, despite his modest income, managed his finances prudently. He lived frugally, consistently saved some of his earnings, and made careful investment decisions based on long-term goals. Over time, his modest nest egg grew, and he achieved financial stability and peace of mind. He found joy in his work, relationships, and connection to the Serenity community.

One day, Amelia returned to Serenity for their high school reunion. She met with Benjamin and shared her accomplishments and struggles. Benjamin, in turn, spoke about his fulfilling life as a guidance counselor and the satisfaction he derived from helping others. As they said, Amelia realized that her knowledge of finance hadn't protected her from making poor financial choices.

Benjamin shared his insights on money intelligence and explained how understanding human behavior and emotions was crucial in making sound financial decisions. He told Amelia that she could achieve a more balanced and fulfilling life by focusing on her emotional well-being and long-term goals. Inspired by Benjamin's wisdom, Amelia decided to reevaluate her financial priorities and seek a deeper understanding of the emotional aspects of money management.

Amelia's journey of self-discovery led her to explore the nuances of financial psychology. She began to understand that financial success was not merely a matter of accumulating wealth but also required emotional intelligence, discipline, and an awareness of one's values and priorities.

With Benjamin's guidance, Amelia gradually transformed her financial habits. She paid off her debts, started retirement savings, and invested in causes that aligned with her values. As a result, she experienced greater satisfaction and happiness in her life.

Meanwhile, Benjamin continued to help the students of Serenity navigate their emotional and financial challenges. He used his understanding of money intelligence to teach them the importance of managing their finances, focusing on long-term well-being and happiness.

The story of Amelia and Benjamin serves as a powerful reminder of the significance of the psychology of money in our lives. It highlights the importance of understanding human behavior, emotions, and values when making financial decisions.

In conclusion, the key to financial success and happiness lies in acknowledging the impact of emotions and psychology on our financial choices. We can achieve a more balanced and fulfilling life by focusing on long-term well-being, cultivating emotional intelligence, and aligning our financial decisions with our values. The story of Amelia and

Benjamin illustrates that financial knowledge alone is insufficient; true financial wisdom comes from understanding and managing the complex interplay between our emotions, behavior, and financial decisions.

Chapter 1: Compounding Power

The butterfly effect teaches us that small actions can have significant consequences. It is the concept that even the slightest movements, like flapping a butterfly's wings, can eventually lead to significant shifts in weather patterns and systems. Chaos theory shows that minor variations in initial conditions can result in widely diverging outcomes.

In a way, the butterfly effect illustrates the power of compounding. Flapping a butterfly's wings may seem insignificant, but over time, that slight movement can create ripples that grow and spread, leading to monumental shifts in the world around us. The idea that small things can have significant effects is accurate in the weather and our daily lives.

As a butterfly's wings can eventually cause a storm, our seemingly small actions and decisions can lead to significant outcomes. Every decision we make, and every step we take, has the potential to create a ripple effect that can impact our lives and the lives of those around us. This is why it's essential to be mindful of our choices, even the seemingly insignificant ones, as they can accumulate and compound into something much more significant.

The power of compounding is not limited to our individual lives but applies to the systems and structures around us. Small changes in one area can create a domino effect that impacts multiple locations and entire communities. This is why it's crucial to consider the long-term consequences of our actions and decisions and take responsibility for our impact on the world.

The butterfly effect shows us that we can create change, even if it starts with something as small as a butterfly's wings. It reminds us that our actions and decisions matter and that we have the potential to make a positive impact on the world through the power of compounding.

When Brian Chesky and Joe Gebbia struggled to pay rent in San Francisco, they rented air mattresses in their living room to conference attendees who had nowhere to stay. This small idea eventually led to the creation of Airbnb, a company that revolutionized the hospitality industry.

Initially, Chesky and Gebbia would spend their days hustling to find new customers, often knocking on doors and handing out flyers. Their efforts paid off as they soon found that many preferred the unique experiences of Airbnb over traditional hotels. Word of mouth quickly spread, and the company's growth compounded.

With the help of co-founder Nathan Blecharczyk, Airbnb continued to innovate and expand, offering more services and experiences to its customers. Today, the company has over 7 million listings in 220 countries, estimated at over $100 billion.

The success of Airbnb is a testament to the power of compounding. What started as a small idea quickly grew into a global phenomenon, all because Chesky and Gebbia dared to take a chance and had the persistence to keep going even when things were tough. Their early efforts, no matter how small, created momentum that continued to build and snowball over time.

Just like the butterfly effect, small actions can have enormous consequences. The key is to keep taking small steps forward and to let the power of compounding work in your favor. Whether you're building a business, learning a new skill, or working on personal growth, remember that every small effort counts and has the potential to create significant results over time.

Ray Dalio's story is one of the most remarkable examples of how compounding power can lead to incredible success. His investment firm, Bridgewater Associates, is now one of the world's largest and most successful hedge funds, with over $150 billion in assets under management. But his success did not come overnight, nor was it a product of luck. Instead, it resulted from decades of hard work, discipline, and a relentless commitment to his principles.

Dalio started investing in the stock market when he was just 12 years old. He was immediately hooked and began studying the market with an intensity few people could match. He would spend hours poring over financial statements, studying the behavior of successful investors, and analyzing market trends. He quickly realized that investing was a hobby and a lifelong passion.

Dalio made several mistakes in his early years, as any new investor would. But he learned from each one, and he used each experience as an opportunity to refine his investment approach. He always sought improvement and wanted more than his current knowledge and skill.

As he got older, Dalio's passion for investing only grew stronger. He went on to study finance in college and then started working on Wall Street. He quickly made a name for himself as a savvy investor, and several top firms soon recruited him. But he always had his sights set on something more significant.

In 1975, Dalio founded Bridgewater Associates with just $5 million in the capital. The firm started small but quickly gained a reputation for its unique investment approach, which emphasized using computer algorithms to identify market trends and opportunities. Over time, the firm's assets grew steadily, and Dalio became one of the most successful investors in the world.

But his success was not just due to his investment approach. It was also a product of his commitment to his principles. Dalio was always guided by a set of core values, which he believed were essential to achieving success in the long run. He was honest and transparent and always put his client's interests ahead of his own. He was also committed to radical transparency, which meant he was always open and honest with his colleagues and clients, even when difficult.

As Bridgewater Associates grew, Dalio's commitment to his principles grew stronger. He created a unique culture at the firm, emphasizing radical transparency, meritocracy, and a willingness to embrace failure. He encouraged his colleagues to challenge each other's ideas and always to be willing to learn from mistakes. This culture helped the firm to attract some of the best talents in the industry, and it became known as a breeding ground for successful investors and entrepreneurs.

Today, Bridgewater Associates is a behemoth in the investment world, with over 1,500 employees and over $150 billion in assets under management. But it all started with one man's passion for investing and unwavering commitment to his principles. Ray Dalio's story is a testament to the power of compounding and the idea that anything is possible with hard work, discipline, and a commitment to your principles.

George Soros is a Hungarian-American investor, businessman, and philanthropist widely regarded as one of the most successful investors in history. His net worth is estimated to be over $8 billion, but his understanding and use of the concept of compounding power set him apart from other successful investors.

Soros began his career in finance as a clerk in a London bank in 1954, and he eventually worked his way up to become a trader and fund manager. In 1969, he founded Soros Fund Management, one of history's most successful hedge funds. Over four decades, Soros generated returns of over 30% per year, making him one of the wealthiest people in the world.

What is the secret to Soros's success? Like Buffett and Dalio, Soros recognized the power of compounding. He understood that small gains, over time, can add up to enormous wealth. But Soros took this concept to another level by using leverage to amplify his returns. He would borrow money to invest in the stock market, betting his investments would appreciate. When they did, he would sell them for a profit and use the proceeds to buy more assets.

But Soros's success wasn't just due to his use of leverage. He was also a master of identifying undervalued assets and investing in them before others caught on. For example, in the 1970s, he invested heavily in Japanese equities, recognizing that the country's economy was on the verge of a massive boom. His investments paid off handsomely, and he made similar bets in other countries and sectors.

Soros's success was not without controversy, however. In the 1990s, he made a massive bet against the British pound, which earned him over $1 billion in profits but also sparked a political firestorm. Critics accused him of using his wealth to manipulate the market and undermine the British economy. Soros defended himself, arguing that he was taking advantage of an overvalued currency and that his actions were in the market's best interest.

Despite the controversy, Soros's success is a testament to the power of compounding. He started with a small sum of money and turned it into a vast fortune through shrewd investing, leveraged bets, and a deep understanding of market trends. His story is a reminder that wealth creation is a slow, steady process that requires patience, discipline, and a long-term perspective.

The growth potential can often be underestimated due to the seeming insignificance of small changes in the beginning. It's the equivalent of looking at a sapling and failing to recognize that it will one day become a mighty oak tree. This phenomenon is not exclusive to investing or natural processes but to all areas of life. We overlook the small, incremental steps that lead to excellent outcomes, focusing only on the result. We see successful people and believe they were always that way rather than acknowledging the hard work and effort they put in for a long time.

We may have all heard stories about the power of compounding interest or how saving in your 20s versus 30s can make a huge difference in your retirement funds. However, how many of us internalize that information and act on it? The truth is, it's easy to dismiss the small changes that can lead to significant growth because we tend to focus only on the final result. It's essential to recognize that growth is a gradual process, and every small decision we make can lead us down a different path.

Our small, incremental steps can add to significant results, whether we're talking about investing, personal relationships, or physical health. We need to be aware of the compounding power of our decisions, recognizing that every action we take will have a ripple effect on our future. It's not about achieving quick success or making dramatic changes; it's about consistently making small, positive changes that will lead us to desired outcomes. So let's start recognizing the power of small steps and taking action towards our goals, one decision at a time.

Consider the story of the Wright brothers. They didn't invent the airplane by making one giant leap forward in aviation technology but rather through a series of minor, iterative improvements that built upon each other. Their early gliders were crude and experimental, but they learned more each time they tested them and made minor adjustments that led to better results.

Similarly, when we examine the success stories of great investors like George Soros or Peter Lynch, we often overlook the power of compounding. It's not just about making suitable investments or being lucky - it's about being consistent and patient, allowing small gains to build upon each other over time.

Yet, our culture often values the quick fix, the overnight success, the one big win that solves everything. We overlook the power of incremental progress and that even minor improvements can add up to incredible outcomes.

Whether we're talking about aviation, investing, or any other field, the power of compounding is always at work. The accumulation of small successes leads to significant breakthroughs, the gradual improvements that add to transformational change. And if we can learn to appreciate the power of the small, to value consistency over flashiness, then we can achieve great things - not just in our investments but in our lives as a whole.

Imagine a time when a single tape reel could hold only 224 kilobytes of data. By the 1960s, mainframes used magnetic tape with a storage capacity of up to 240 megabytes. In the 1970s, hard disk drives began to appear, with capacities of around 5 megabytes. By the 1980s, personal computers were commonplace, and a typical hard drive could store about 20-30 megabytes. But then, technology advanced at an exponential rate. In 1995, a computer hard drive could store 1 gigabyte of data. In 2000, it was up to 20 gigabytes. By 2005, the capacity had grown to 200 gigabytes. And then, things started to get crazy. In 2010, hard drives with a total of 2 terabytes were available. Just five years later, that number had exploded to 10 terabytes. And in 2021, getting your hands on a hard drive with a staggering 100 terabytes of storage capacity is possible.

The lesson is that minor, incremental technological improvements can lead to incredible results. Over time, what starts as a single reel of tape or a 5-megabyte hard drive can turn into a 100-terabyte behemoth. It's easy to overlook the power of exponential growth, but the numbers don't lie. And just as the capacity of hard drives has grown exponentially, so too has the potential of technology to transform our lives in ways we can hardly imagine.

In the 1970s, the average weight of a cell phone was over 2.5 pounds, costing over $3,000 (adjusted for inflation). By the 1990s, the average weight had dropped to under a pound, and the cost had decreased to around $1,000. Then, things started to pick up the pace. In the early 2000s, flip phones became the norm, weighing in just a few ounces and costing a few hundred dollars. By the late 2000s, smartphones had taken over, with the first iPhone weighing just 4.8 ounces and costing $499. And then, just like with hard drives, the explosion happened. Today, smartphones can weigh as little as 5.5 ounces and cost as little as $99, with some of the more high-end models weighing just over 6 ounces and costing over $1,000. These devices' processing power and capabilities have also exponentially increased, with some models boasting more power than the computers used to send humans to the moon in the 1960s. The rate of technological advancement has been staggering, and what was once unthinkable is now a reality.

In 1983, the first commercially available cell phone weighed over 2 pounds and cost around $4,000. It could only make and receive phone calls and had a battery life of about 30 minutes. By the 1990s, cell phones became more affordable and accessible but were still relatively primitive, with limited features and functionality. The Nokia 1011, released in 1992, was one of the first mass-market mobile phones and could store up to 99 phone numbers.

Then, in the early 2000s, things started to take off. They introduced smartphones, like the BlackBerry and the iPhone, bringing new capabilities and connectivity to mobile devices. By 2010, smartphones had become ubiquitous, with millions of people using them for everything from email and messaging to social media and streaming video.

As technology continued to evolve, so did the capabilities of smartphones. By 2019, the average smartphone had a more powerful processor than the computer used to land Apollo 11 on the moon. They had high-resolution touchscreens, facial recognition, and the ability to support augmented reality applications. Some models even had foldable screens and 5G connectivity.

What started as a bulky and expensive gadget for making phone calls has transformed into a pocket-sized computer that can connect us with people and information from anywhere in the world. And just like the hard drive example, this transformation happened gradually, with each small advancement building upon the last to create something truly remarkable.

Investing is often seen as a game of chasing the highest returns, but the secret to success may lie in a simple phrase: patience pays off. It's easy to become enamored with hitting it big with one big investment or chasing the latest hot stock tip. But the truth is, those one-off successes are often the exception rather than the rule. The key to long-term success in investing is finding solid investments that can provide consistent returns over time and sticking with them for the long haul.

The power of compounding drives long-term growth in investments, which means being patient and disciplined enough to let your assets grow over time. It's only sometimes the most exciting approach, and it won't make you an overnight millionaire, but it's the strategy that has proven most effective over the long haul.

Of course, it's easier said than done. It's hard to resist the temptation to chase quick profits or panic when the market is downturned. But those who can stay the course, who can be patient and wait for their investments to grow, are the ones who are most likely to come out ahead in the long run.

So if you're looking for the secret to investing success, look no further than patience. It may not be as glamorous as some other investment strategies, but it's the one that has stood the test of time and that can truly help you build long-term wealth.

Chapter 2: No One is Right or Wrong

Each person's relationship with money is unique, depending on their upbringing, surroundings, and life experiences. Our parents, communities, and culture instill specific values and beliefs about money in us from birth.

For some, money represents security and stability, a way to provide for their family and ensure a comfortable future. For others, money is a source of freedom and opportunity, a means to pursue their passions and dreams.

But despite these differences, one thing is clear: the way we view money is shaped by our experiences. And because those experiences are unique to each individual, our views on money can vary wildly from person to person.

For example, imagine two people born in different parts of the world, raised in other economic conditions, and exposed to different cultures. One person might see money as a limited resource that needs to be carefully managed and saved, while another might see it as a beautiful and limitless way to get what they want.

Even within a single country or community, people's experiences with money can be vastly different.

Someone who grew up in poverty might view financial risk and reward differently than someone who grew up in affluence. Similarly, someone who experienced a recession in their early years might be more cautious with their money than someone who's only known economic growth and stability.

All of these experiences shape our beliefs and behaviors around money, and what may seem irrational or foolish to one person may be perfectly logical to another. That's why it's important to remember that there's no "right" way to manage your money. What works for one person may not work for another, and vice versa.

So the next time you hear about someone making a questionable financial decision, remember that their perspective and experiences are likely very different from yours. By acknowledging and respecting these differences, we can learn to understand and care about the financial decisions of others and be better prepared to make our own.

Mary grew up in a low-income family in a rural town. Her parents worked multiple jobs to make ends meet, and money was always a struggle. They lived in a small house without luxuries, and Mary learned early on to save every penny. She worked part-time jobs throughout high school and college to help her family and eventually became a successful accountant. Money is significant to her; she values saving for a rainy day above all else.

On the other hand, John was born into a wealthy family in the city. His parents were excellent at business and taught him to like taking risks and investing. They gave him all the chances they could, and he went to the best schools and got an excellent education. John became a stockbroker and quickly became known for his bold investment strategies. To him, money is a means to an end, a way to create more opportunities and experiences in life.

Mary and John may be successful financially, but their views on money could be similar. Mary saves every penny she earns, while John is willing to take significant risks to make big rewards.

Sarah grew up in a small town in a middle-class family. Her parents were teachers, and they valued education and hard work above all else. They only talked about money a little, but Sarah learned early on that saving and investing were necessary for her future. She worked hard in school, went to college, and became a successful lawyer. Money is essential to her, but not the most important thing in her life.

On the other hand, Tom grew up in a wealthy family in the suburbs. His parents were successful entrepreneurs who owned multiple businesses. They instilled in Tom a love of entrepreneurship and taking risks. Tom dropped out of college to start his own business, eventually becoming successful. To him, money is a way to gain power and influence worldwide.

Sarah and Tom may be successful financially, but their views on money differ. Sarah values hard work and education, while Tom values entrepreneurship and risk-taking.

During the dot-com boom of the late 1990s, many young entrepreneurs made millions seemingly overnight, while others watched their retirement savings evaporate in the resulting bust. Take two people who started their careers at the same time. One landed a job at a high-flying startup and watched their stock options soar in value, while the other worked at a traditional company that offered a modest but stable salary. The first person enjoyed exotic vacations, designer clothes, and a flashy sports car in the following years. In contrast, the second person scrimped, saved, and invested steadily in a diversified portfolio. But when the dot-com bubble burst, the first person was left with worthless stock options and a pile of debt, while the second person had a healthy retirement account and a paid-off mortgage. The different experiences left each person with a fundamentally different understanding of money.

Or consider two people who grew up in the same town but on opposite sides of the tracks. One came from a wealthy family and never had to worry about money, while the other came from a single-parent household and worked part-time jobs to help pay the bills. When they reached adulthood, the first person had access to every opportunity money could buy—private schools, Ivy League colleges, and a network of powerful connections—while the second person had to claw their way up from the bottom, working hard to earn scholarships and break into elite circles. Their vastly different experiences with money and privilege shaped their attitudes and beliefs about what it takes to succeed in life.

The enigma of fear and uncertainty presents a challenge for everyone. We can read about economic disasters, war, or pandemics, but we can only fully grasp the psychological impact of these events once we have lived through them ourselves. Each person's experience is unique and shaped by their background, upbringing, and culture. This inevitably colors how they view and respond to the world around them. A person who has lived through a traumatic event might consider the future with trepidation, while another who has been spared such an experience might be more optimistic.

Studying history can provide some insight into past events, but it needs to fully capture their emotional toll on individuals. For example, we can look at the data on the stock market's performance during a financial crisis, but it cannot simulate the feeling of dread that comes with seeing your investments plummet in value.

Our own experiences often limit our knowledge of the world. The famous author and philosopher Albert Camus once said, "You cannot create an experience. You must undergo it." Through experiencing events firsthand, we can gain a deeper understanding of their actual impact. This is true for everyone, no matter how intelligent or well-read. We're all limited by what we've done and seen, and we must accept that our understanding of the world changes based on what we've done and seen.

53% of Americans said they were worried about money in the past year, according to a 2019 survey by the National Endowment for Financial Education. The survey also found that almost nine out of ten Americans feel stressed about money. Saving and debt are the two biggest sources of financial stress.

These statistics highlight financial stress's emotional toll on individuals and how personal experiences shape one's relationship with money. It's one thing to read about the effects of a recession or market crash, but it's another to live through it and experience the uncertainty and fear that come with it.

Also, the survey shows that many Americans still need help with basic money management skills, despite efforts to improve financial literacy and education. For example, the survey found that nearly two-thirds of Americans do not have a written budget, and only 49% of respondents reported having an emergency fund.

These results show how important it is to understand how personal experiences affect financial behaviors and decisions. As the survey suggests, financial stress and anxiety are prevalent issues that lack basic financial management skills can compound. To improve one's financial situation, one must understand the technical parts of personal finance and be aware of and deal with the emotional and mental factors at play.

To better understand how different economic environments can shape investment perspectives, we interviewed four individuals who grew up in vastly different periods.

The first person, Jack, was born in the late 1930s during the Great Depression. Growing up in a family that struggled to make ends meet, Jack was taught from a young age to be frugal and to save every penny. He developed a deep distrust of the stock market and preferred to invest in tangible assets such as real estate and gold. His experiences shaped Jack's investment strategy during his formative years and the lasting impact of the Great Depression.

The second person, Rachel, was born in the 1950s during economic prosperity in the United States. Her family was firmly middle class and enjoyed a comfortable lifestyle. Rachel was taught to invest in stocks and bonds from a young age and was encouraged to pursue a college education and a career. Her investment strategy is rooted in a belief in the long-term growth potential of the stock market and a focus on building wealth through a diversified portfolio.

The third person, Maria, was born in the 1980s during economic uncertainty and instability. Her family immigrated to the United States from a developing country and struggled to make a living. Maria was taught to be cautious with money and to save as much as possible. She hesitated to invest in the stock market and preferred keeping her savings in a high-yield account. Her experiences influence Maria's investment strategy as an immigrant and her desire for financial stability.

The fourth person, David, was born in the early 2000s and came of age during rapid technological advancement and economic globalization. David's investment strategy is shaped by his belief in the power of technology and innovation. He is bullish on emerging markets and new blockchain and artificial intelligence technologies. David's investment philosophy is influenced by globalization's unprecedented opportunities and technology's transformative power.

These four individuals demonstrate how different economic environments can shape investment perspectives. Jack's experiences during the Great Depression instilled a deep distrust of the stock market. At the same time, Rachel's comfortable upbringing and economic prosperity led her to believe in the long-term potential of stocks and bonds. Maria's experiences as an immigrant and the economy's instability have taught her to be careful with money. On the other hand, David's views on investing have been shaped by his exposure to new technologies and globalization. Understanding how different economic environments shape investment perspectives is crucial to a successful strategy.

In a small village in Southeast Asia, a factory is a beacon of hope for hundreds of workers. The factory is the largest employer in the region, where Linh, a young worker, spends her days stitching together clothes for Western markets.

Linh feels grateful for her job despite the long hours, low pay, and dangerous working conditions. She knows that if she were still living in her rural village, she would struggle to make ends meet without hoping for a better future.

When a Western journalist visited the factory to report on the working conditions, she was appalled at what she saw. The factory was hot and humid, with no air conditioning, and workers sat for hours on end without breaks. The journalist interviewed Linh, who spoke about the harsh conditions and long hours.

The journalist asked Linh if she thought the factory should be shut down or if workers should go on strike. But to her surprise, Linh replied that she was grateful for her job and didn't want the factory to close.

Linh explained that she had grown up in poverty and that the factory had allowed her to improve her life. She knew her job wasn't perfect, but it was a stepping stone toward a better future.

Linh's response humbled the journalist. She realized that working conditions were more complex than she had initially thought. While the factory certainly had room for improvement, it provided jobs and opportunities that might not otherwise exist.

Linh's story serves as a reminder that the global economy is a complicated web of interconnected factors. While we should always strive for better working conditions and fair wages, we must also recognize the role of factories like hers in lifting people out of poverty and providing a path to a better life.

Money is a topic that has been around for centuries, yet the concepts of saving and investing that are so crucial to our financial well-being are relatively new. It is vital to recognize how recent these ideas are to understand why money decisions can be so challenging and why people often make mistakes.

For example, consider the idea of retirement. Even though we take it for granted now, the idea that people should be able to rest after years of hard work is new. The concept of retirement as we know it today is only a few generations old.

Before the early 20th century, retirement was not a common practice. Many people worked until they were no longer physically able to and then relied on their families for support in their old age. Setting aside money for retirement was separate from most people's financial plans.

It wasn't until the Great Depression of the 1930s that the concept of retirement began to take hold in the United States. The government's creation of Social Security, which provided a safety net for elderly Americans who could no longer work, was a significant factor in this shift. Suddenly, people had a financial incentive to plan for their retirement years, and many began to do so.

However, even with the creation of Social Security, retirement, as we know it today, was still a distant dream for most people. It was in the 1970s that the 401(k) concept was introduced, which allowed workers to set aside money for retirement on a tax-deferred basis. This made it easier and more accessible for people to save for retirement and helped to solidify the idea that retirement was something that everyone should plan for.

Today, retirement savings are crucial to many Americans' financial plans. With $27 trillion in U.S. retirement accounts at the end of 2018, retirement savings are a major driver of the typical investor's saving and investing decisions. Yet it is important to remember that these concepts are still relatively new, and many people worldwide do not have access to retirement savings programs.

Understanding the history of retirement and the development of retirement savings programs can help us to appreciate just how far we have come and how important it is to continue to plan for our financial future.

The statistics paint a concerning picture of Americans' retirement savings habits. According to a survey conducted by the Federal Reserve in 2019, nearly one in four adults had no retirement savings or pension. Among those with retirement savings, the median amount was only $60,000. This is far below the amount needed to provide a comfortable retirement.

Furthermore, the survey found that retirement savings are closely tied to income and education. Adults with higher incomes and more education tend to have more retirement savings than those with lower incomes and less education. For example, the median retirement savings for a household earning $100,000 or more per year was $400,000, compared to only $25,000 for a family earning less than $40,000 per year.

The study also revealed that Americans need to save more for retirement. Experts generally recommend saving at least 10-15% of income for retirement, but the survey found that the median amount saved among those who did save was only 7% of their income.

Additionally, only 37% of non-retired adults think they are on track with their retirement savings goals.

The survey shows that many Americans need to be adequately prepared for retirement. With proper savings and planning, they may avoid financial struggles later. Individuals must take a proactive approach to retirement savings, and policymakers must consider policies promoting retirement savings and security.

Money makes us all do crazy things

Our actions are dictated by our life's offerings

What may look absurd to one may be logical to another. We each live in our world with experiences that differ from each other.

No one is insane or out of their mind

Our choices are guided by what we have left behind

The choices we make may seem odd to some

But they are based on our stories and the life that we've come from

Money is an enigma that we are all trying to solve

With the hope that one day, it will help us evolve

Our decision-making is guided by what we know

And the experiences we've had that helped us grow

So let's not judge others for what they do with their wealth

For their journey is not ours, and we must remind ourselves

That we all have our own unique life to live

And the choices we make are based on the experiences we have.

Chapter 3: The Importance of Saving Money

The world is changing rapidly, and as our population grows, we face new challenges in consuming resources. Technological advances give us new ways to save energy and lessen our environmental impact.

One of the most exciting things in the past few years is the rise of less-energy technologies. These innovations, from LED lighting to electric vehicles, are helping us save money and resources in ways we never thought possible.

For example, LED lighting uses a fraction of the energy of traditional incandescent bulbs while lasting up to 25 times longer. This helps us reduce our carbon footprint and save us money on energy bills.

Similarly, the increasing affordability and accessibility of electric vehicles make them a viable option for consumers. With the cost of batteries and other components decreasing, electric cars are also falling, making them a more attractive option for environmentally conscious drivers.

These technological advances are not just good for our wallets and the planet - they are also a testament to the power of human innovation. By embracing new technologies and making conscious choices about our consumption, we can pave the way for a brighter, more sustainable future.

Regarding our finances, it's easy to get caught up in the allure of high returns and investment strategies. But the truth is, the world of finance is shrouded in uncertainty, and there's no guarantee that any particular investment will deliver the returns we hope for.

Fortunately, one aspect of our finances is entirely within control: our personal savings rate. By being mindful of our spending and practicing frugality, we can conserve and efficiently manage our finances, regardless of market conditions.

At its core, wealth is simply the accumulation of what's left over after we've spent what we earn. And while a high income can make building wealth easier, it's not a prerequisite. However, a commitment to saving and a willingness to live within our means is essential.

Prioritizing our savings rate over our income can be a more effective way to build wealth in the long run. After all, while investment returns may be uncertain, the benefits of saving and frugality are guaranteed. Focusing on what we can control and practicing good financial habits can build a solid foundation for our economic future.

Our personal savings rate is a critical component of our financial well-being. While investment returns and market conditions may be uncertain, our ability to conserve and efficiently manage our finances is entirely within our control. By prioritizing our savings rate and living within our means, we can build wealth and achieve financial stability, regardless of our income level.

Consider this situation - you and I possess an equivalent net worth. But, there is a crucial contrast between us. You have a talent for investing, with an ability to achieve an impressive 15% annual return, while I can only manage a modest 7%. Nevertheless, there is a defining aspect where I excel - I am highly efficient with my finances and require only half the resources you need to find happiness. In contrast, your standard of living grows in tandem with your wealth.

Interestingly, despite your prowess in investing, I am in a better position than you. I can derive more benefits from my investments despite lower returns. Also, learning to be happy with a smaller income creates a big gap between what we want and what we have. This gap resembles the one that results from a salary increase, but it is a gap that is easier to bridge and well within our control.

It's interesting how closely our financial satisfaction is tied to how well we manage our resources. It is not always about how much wealth one accumulates but how resourcefully we use what we have. Ultimately, being content with less can be more valuable than constantly striving for more.

Consider the significance of a high savings rate - it implies having lower expenses than you could potentially have. With lower expenses, your savings can stretch further than if you spent more. Now, take a moment to reflect on the concept of investment outperformance. It takes millions of hours of research and billions of dollars of effort from professionals to achieve even the slightest percentage-point increase in annual returns.

Comparing these two concepts makes what's truly valuable and worthy of pursuit evident. Some investors grind for hours, dedicating themselves to increasing their returns by even a fraction of a percentage point. However, several percentage points of lifestyle expenses can be reduced with significantly less effort.

This begs the question - why do we emphasize chasing meager investment returns while ignoring the savings that could be gained by managing our expenses better? It's a curious problem that warrants further exploration.

The answer may lie in our priorities and choices. Are we willing to sacrifice present-day pleasures to secure a brighter financial future? Or do we prioritize instant gratification over long-term stability? The option is ours to make, but it's essential to keep in mind that every penny saved today has the potential to grow exponentially in the future.

What matters more in the grand scheme - pursuing a minuscule investment outperformance or realizing potential savings that could lead to significant financial success and stability? The answer may not be as clear-cut as we'd like, but it's worth considering.

In today's consumer-driven world, it is easy to lose sight of what matters regarding personal finance. We are constantly bombarded with advertisements for the latest gadgets, fashion trends, and luxury items that promise to improve our lives. However, beyond a certain point, spending money on material possessions is less about fulfilling our needs and more about satisfying our ego.

The pressure to keep up with the Joneses can be overwhelming, and it can be challenging to resist the urge to spend money on things we don't need. However, we must cultivate humility and learn to live within our means to achieve financial security and stability.

One of the most potent ways to increase our savings is to redefine our definition of success.

Instead of measuring our worth in terms of our possessions and wealth, we should focus on what matters - our relationships, our health, and our personal growth. We can escape materialism by changing priorities and finding more happiness and satisfaction.

It is important to remember that financial success is not necessarily about having a high income or amassing vast wealth. Some of the most financially secure individuals have learned to live and prioritize their needs over their wants. They understand that true happiness and contentment come from within and that material possessions are not a substitute for personal fulfillment and purpose.

The key to achieving lasting financial success lies in cultivating humility and focusing on what matters in life. By redefining our definition of success and prioritizing our needs over our wants, we can break free from the cycle of materialism and achieve greater satisfaction and contentment in our lives.

For many people, saving money is something they do with a specific goal, whether buying a new car or saving for retirement. And while having a target to aim for can be helpful, it's important to remember that saving doesn't always have to be about reaching a specific milestone.

Saving for the sake of saving can be a powerful way to give yourself more options and flexibility in life. By building up a solid savings cushion, you can protect yourself against the unexpected and be better prepared to weather life's inevitable storms.

But the benefits of saving go beyond just financial security. The intangible rewards of having money in the bank can be just as valuable - if not more so - than the tangible things money can buy. Savings can give you freedom and control over your life, allowing you to take risks and make choices on your terms.

One of the most potent benefits of saving is the gift of time. By building up your savings, you can create a buffer that gives you the space and freedom to think, reflect, and make choices that align with your values and goals. Rather than being forced to make decisions in the heat of the moment, you can take your time, weigh your options, and make choices that truly reflect who you are.

There is a growing trend towards precision medicine - an approach that tailors medical treatment to an individual's genetic makeup, lifestyle, and environment. One of the critical challenges of precision medicine is making it accessible to all patients, regardless of their socioeconomic background.

Recently, a study was conducted on the cost-effectiveness of precision medicine for patients with lung cancer. The study found that while precision medicine was more expensive than standard chemotherapy, it led to better outcomes and fewer adverse effects. However, the study also found that the cost of precision medicine was often a barrier for patients, particularly those with low incomes.

This study highlights the importance of saving money and preparing for unexpected expenses. In the case of precision medicine, having savings can mean the difference between receiving life-saving treatment or not. This is just one example of how saving money can significantly impact our lives and well-being.

Jack worked as a software engineer for a company for over a decade. He loved his job and was passionate about coding. He had a comfortable salary and enjoyed a good life with his family.

One day, Jack's company announced that they were planning to lay off several employees due to a downturn in the economy. Jack was devastated to learn that his job was one of the ones on the chopping block. Even though Jack had been with the company for a long time and worked hard, he suddenly lost his job.

But Jack was a savvy saver. He had set aside some of his monthly income for years and built a solid emergency fund. When he learned he would be laid off, Jack initially panicked. But he quickly realized that his savings gave him the flexibility and security he needed to weather the storm.

Thanks to his savings, Jack was able to take some time off to regroup and figure out his next steps. He spent a few months exploring job opportunities and networking with other professionals in his field. And while it wasn't easy, Jack eventually landed a new job that he loved even more than his old one.

Looking back on his experience, Jack realized that his savings had been the key to his success. Without the financial cushion he had built up, he would have been forced to take the first job that came his way - even if it wasn't a good fit for him. But because he had savings, Jack could take his time, explore his options, and make choices aligned with his values and goals.

From that day forward, Jack prioritized his savings, recognizing that they were the key to his financial well-being and security. He encouraged his friends and family to do the same, knowing that savings in an ever-changing world were the best way to prepare for the future.

One study by the American Psychological Association found that individuals with higher levels of financial stress were more likely to experience mental health issues such as depression and anxiety. The study surveyed over 1,000 adults in the United States and found that those with low levels of savings were more likely to report symptoms of anxiety and depression, even when controlling for other factors such as income level.

The study also found that having control over one's finances was necessary for mental health. Individuals who reported feeling more in control of their finances were less likely to experience symptoms of depression and anxiety.

This is supported by other research showing a link between financial stress and poor mental health. A study published in the Journal of Financial Therapy found that individuals with high levels of financial stress were more likely to report symptoms of depression, anxiety, and other mental health issues.

The link between savings and mental health is likely due to a sense of security and control that comes with having financial stability. Individuals with enough savings to cover unexpected expenses and emergencies are less likely to feel stressed and anxious about their finances. This can lead to a healthier overall mental state and a better quality of life.

In life's uncertain, shifting sands,
We all must learn to take a stand,
And build a fortress strong and grand,
With savings that we've safely planned.
For in this world of constant change,
Our futures often rearrange,
And though we try to stay in range,
It's hard to know what lies in range.
But with a nest egg safe and sound,
We'll stand on solid, stable ground,
And when life's challenges come around,
We'll be equipped to stand our ground.
For savings aren't just money stowed,
But freedom from life's heavy load,
A chance to find a different mode,
And live a life that's worth the code.
So let us save with all our might,
And build a future that shines bright,
With confidence and with delight,
And the joy that lasts both day and night.

Chapter 4: Being Reasonable or Rational

In the depths of the Great Depression in the 1930s, the US faced one of its most severe economic crises. The country urgently needed urgent action, with millions unemployed and in widespread poverty.

Franklin D. Roosevelt, who had been elected President in 1932, faced enormous pressure from both liberal and conservative voices on how to address the crisis. Some advocated for a purely rational laissez-faire approach, while others pushed for a more radical socialist program.

But Roosevelt recognized that the situation called for a more reasonable approach that combined elements of both ideologies while maintaining the principles of a capitalist market economy.

He and his administration developed a series of policies that came to be known as the New Deal, which aimed to provide government relief and support for those affected by the economic crisis, while also promoting economic growth and recovery.

The New Deal programs included public works projects, labor protections, agricultural subsidies, and financial reforms. While the New Deal was not without controversy, it represented a reasonable response to the complex realities of the situation at the time.

Roosevelt's decision to choose a reasonable approach was based on his understanding of the context of the situation. He recognized the need for urgent action to address the severe economic crisis while balancing government intervention and market-based solutions.

The New Deal policies implemented by Roosevelt's administration have been widely credited with helping to bring the US out of the Great Depression and have had a lasting impact on American society and politics.

Roosevelt's ability to choose a reasonable approach in the face of competing ideologies and pressures is a testament to his leadership and pragmatism. The New Deal is a powerful example of how choosing to be reasonable, rather than purely rational or ideological, can lead to positive outcomes even in the most challenging circumstances.

In investment theory, many mathematical models and equations are designed to guide investment decisions. These models are meant to be completely logical, taking into account all the available data and avoiding emotional biases as much as possible.

However, in the real world, people are emotional beings, and factors beyond pure rationality often influence their investment decisions. Fear, greed, and social pressure can all influence investment decisions, leading to choices that are not entirely rational.

But there is another way to approach investment decisions, one that considers the context in which they are being made. This approach involves choosing to be reasonable instead of purely rational.

Being reasonable in investment decision-making means recognizing that mathematical models and equations are essential but not the only consideration. Context-specific factors such as personal risk tolerance, investment goals, and financial circumstances are just as crucial in making a sound investment decision.

Consider the story of John, a successful businessman who had built up a considerable portfolio of investments over the years. John was known for being a rational thinker and always made investment decisions based on the latest data and mathematical models.

But one day, John found himself facing a significant personal crisis. His daughter had been diagnosed with a rare medical condition, and he was struggling to find the money to pay for her treatments.

Even though the mathematical models and equations suggested otherwise, John reasonably decided to sell some of his investments to pay for his daughter's medical care. This decision was not purely rational but the right choice for John.

By choosing to be reasonable instead of purely rational, John could make a decision aligned with his values and priorities. This approach allowed him to balance logical analysis with emotional considerations and context-specific factors, leading to a more successful and satisfying outcome.

Mike is a successful businessman who has worked hard to build a comfortable nest egg. Mike has a mortgage on his home, but with a large amount of cash at his disposal, he's now wondering whether to pay off his mortgage or invest the money.

From a purely rational standpoint, it would make more sense for John to invest the money in a diversified portfolio of stocks and bonds. After all, the rate of return on his investments would likely be higher than the interest rate on his mortgage, making it more financially beneficial to invest the money rather than pay off his mortgage.

However, Mike is not just a purely rational thinker. He recognizes debt-free's emotional and psychological benefits and the peace of mind of knowing he owns his home. He's also uncomfortable taking on more risk by investing his money in the stock market.

Mike's situation is familiar. Many people face the same decision between paying off their mortgage or investing their money, and the answer is only sometimes purely rational. For many, paying off their mortgage is a more reasonable approach, considering emotional, psychological, and financial factors.

For example, consider Sarah, a recent widow who had inherited a significant amount of money from her husband's estate. Sarah had a mortgage on her home but decided to pay it off with the inheritance money rather than invest it in the stock market.

Sarah's decision was not purely rational, as the rate of return on her investments would likely have been higher than the interest rate on her mortgage. However, Sarah recognized debt-free's emotional and psychological benefits, especially during difficult times. She also felt more comfortable with a stable and predictable investment than one involving more risk.

The decision to pay off a mortgage with a large amount of cash is a personal one considering a range of factors beyond pure rationality. While investing the money may make more financial sense in some cases, the emotional and psychological benefits of being debt-free and having peace of mind can be just as significant for some people. They choose to be reasonable rather than purely rational by taking a holistic approach to the decision considering financial and emotional factors.

In a 2015 paper titled "*The Rationality of Risky Stocks: Evidence from Experimental Asset Markets,*" authors Guillaume Fréchette and Alessandro Lizzeri conducted a study to investigate how people make investment decisions in experimental asset markets.

The study found that while it may seem rational on paper to pick risky stocks or investment portfolios based on mathematical models and data analysis, people's emotions and psychology often play a significant role in investment decision-making.

The study gave participants a set amount of money to invest in asset markets. The markets were designed to mimic real-world stock markets, with participants able to buy and sell stocks based on their perceived value.

The study's results showed that while participants were initially drawn to risky stocks that promised high returns, they were also highly influenced by emotions such as fear and regret. When their investments performed poorly, participants tended to become more risk-averse, selling off their stocks even if the underlying data suggested that they were undervalued.

This behavior is known as "loss aversion," a psychological phenomenon where people tend to place more weight on losses than gains when making decisions. Loss aversion can lead people to make suboptimal investment decisions, selling off stocks at a loss even if the long-term prospects of the investment are sound.

The study concludes that the rationality of risky stocks may be true in theory. Still, it may need to be more practical and reasonable in practice when the emotions and psychology of investors are taken into account.

Investing decisions are often based on a complex mix of things beyond pure logic, such as personal values, feelings, and social pressures.

The study suggests that choosing to be reasonable, rather than purely rational, when making investment decisions may lead to better outcomes by considering the complex realities of human behavior and psychology.

Maria is a middle-aged American investor who has invested in the stock market for many years. Maria knows adding small, mid-cap, and international stocks to her portfolio is a good idea. However, despite the potential benefits of these investment strategies, Maria tends to stick with large-cap and domestic stocks.

Why does Maria make this choice, despite the potential financial benefits of diversification? The answer lies in her preferences and emotions.

According to a 2019 survey by Ally Invest, a leading investment management firm, many American investors like Maria choose to invest in large-cap and domestic stocks because they feel more familiar and comfortable. In the survey, nearly 70% of investors cited familiarity as the top reason for investing in domestic stocks.

Additionally, the survey found that emotions play a significant role in investment decision-making. More than half of investors surveyed said that fear or anxiety had caused them to sell stocks at some point, even if the underlying data suggested that the stocks were still a good investment.

This behavior is not purely rational, as selling stocks due to fear or anxiety can lead to missed investment opportunities and lower returns. However, it's understandable, given the complex interplay of factors that influence investment decisions.

For Maria, her preference for large-cap and domestic stocks may be driven by her familiarity with these investments and her desire for stability and predictability in her portfolio. While diversifying her portfolio with small and mid-cap stocks and international stocks may offer potentially higher returns in the long term, it may also introduce more risk and uncertainty, which may not align with Maria's values and goals.

One recent psychological theory that explains the behavior of being reasonable, rather than purely rational, in investment decision-making, is behavioral finance.

Behavioral finance is a relatively new field of study that combines principles of traditional finance with insights from psychology to understand better how people make financial decisions. The theory suggests that people are only sometimes rational decision-makers regarding financial matters, as emotions, biases, and other psychological factors can influence their choices.

One of the fundamental tenets of behavioral finance is loss aversion, a concept we touched on earlier. Loss aversion refers to people's tendency to place more weight on losses than gains when making decisions. For example, if an investor sees that their investment has decreased in value, they may become more risk-averse and sell off their stocks, even if the long-term prospects of the investment are sound.

Another important concept in behavioral finance is the availability heuristic, which suggests that people overestimate the likelihood of easily remembered or recalled events. For example, suppose an investor remembers a news story about a company experiencing financial difficulties. In that case, they may be more likely to sell off their stocks, even if the underlying data suggests that the company is still a good investment.

These and other concepts in behavioral finance help explain why people may choose to be reasonable rather than purely rational when making investment decisions. Investors can make better-informed choices that align with their goals and circumstances by considering the emotional and psychological factors influencing decision-making.

In a 2016 study titled "*Investing Under Social Influence: Evidence from the Stock Recommendations of TV Pundits,*" authors Brad Barber and Terrance Odean investigated the impact of social influence on investment decision-making.

The study looked at the stock recommendations of well-known TV pundits and found that investors usually took their advice, even if it wasn't based on sound financial data or analysis. The study suggests that social influence can significantly influence investment decision-making, leading investors to make suboptimal choices.

The study is an example of how social factors can impact investment decisions, a key concept in behavioral finance. Investors may be influenced by the opinions of others in their social network, including financial experts and media personalities, even when these opinions may not be based on sound financial analysis.

This behavior is not purely rational, as investors may be swayed by social factors rather than considering the long-term fundamentals of an investment. However, it's understandable, given the complex interplay of psychological factors that influence investment decision-making.

The study demonstrates the importance of considering social and cultural factors when making investment decisions, a key concept in behavioral finance. By recognizing the impact of social influence on investment decision-making, investors can make better-informed choices that align with their personal goals and values.

Overall, the study is a compelling example of how behavioral finance can help explain why people are only sometimes rational decision-makers regarding financial matters. By considering the emotional, cognitive, and social factors that influence investment decisions, investors can make better-informed choices that are more reasonable and aligned with their personal goals and values.

Tim Cook is known for his sharp business acumen and ability to make decisions based on data analysis and market trends. However, Cook also recognizes the importance of being reasonable rather than purely rational in certain situations.

In 2013, Cook gave a significant portion of his fortune to charity. Cook's decision was not based purely on rational reasons but on personal values and a desire to impact the world positively.

Cook's decision was motivated in part by his desire to honor the memory of his late uncle, who had never married or had children and was a crucial influence in Cook's life. Cook recognized that his uncle had instilled a strong sense of values and a desire to impact the world positively.

Cook's decision to give away his fortune was not purely rational, as it did not necessarily provide the highest financial return for himself or Apple. However, it was reasonable and aligned with Cook's values and goals. Cook recognized that business success was not just about making the highest financial returns but also about positively impacting the world and living a life guided by solid values.

Chapter 5: Enough is Enough

I hung out with my friend Edwin Wang one time. Edwin and I have been friends for a long time, and we usually have deep conversations about life and money. We were sitting in a cozy coffee shop, and I couldn't help but notice how happy and content Edwin looked. So, I decided to ask him about his financial situation.

"Edwin, I have to ask you, how are you so happy with your financial situation? I mean, your income is not high at all, yet you always seem content and happy."

Edwin took a sip of his coffee and smiled at me. "I used to be like you, always chasing more money, always trying to earn more. But then I realized that there is more to life than just money. I realized that I had enough, and I was content with what I had."

I looked at Edwin skeptically. "But how did you manage to overcome the distraction of money? I mean, money is essential to survive, right?"

Edwin nodded. "Of course, money is important, but it's not everything. I learned to prioritize my needs and wants. I started to focus on the things that brought me happiness, like spending time with my family, traveling, and pursuing my hobbies. I stopped chasing after the latest gadgets, expensive clothes, and luxury items. I realized that I had enough, and that was more than enough for me."

I was intrigued by Edwin's philosophy, and I started to think about my own life. I realized I had been caught up in the rat race of earning more money, buying more things, and trying to keep up with the Joneses. But Edwin's words struck a chord, and I realized I needed to change my priorities.

After the conversation, I was walking down the street, lost in thought about the conversation I had just had with Edwin. He had seemed so content with his life despite not having a lot of money, and it had left me wondering why so many people struggled with being satisfied with enough.

As I walked, I noticed a man in a suit rush past me, his eyes glued to his phone. He seemed completely absorbed in whatever he was reading, oblivious to the world around him. It made me wonder, was he among the many people who had become a slave to money and material possessions?

I continued down the street, my mind racing with questions. Why did people find it so hard to be content with what they had? What was it about money that drove people always to want more? Could society have put too much emphasis on wealth and success, making it difficult for people to find contentment in their lives?

I walked past a designer clothing store and noticed a group of young people taking selfies in front of the window. They were all wearing expensive clothes and seemed completely absorbed in their reflection. It made me wonder, did they believe that material possessions would bring them happiness and fulfillment?

As I continued walking, I noticed a woman sitting on a park bench, staring into space. She seemed lost in thought, and I wondered what was on her mind. Was she one of the many people trapped in the cycle of always wanting more, never satisfied with what she had?

It was clear that many factors were at play regarding people's inability to find contentment and be happy with enough. Whether it was societal pressures, human nature, or the belief that material possessions equaled happiness, many distractions made it difficult for people to adopt the concept of being content with what they had, just like Edwin did.

As I walked home, I couldn't help but wonder how we could break free from these distractions and learn to be content with enough. But for now, all I could do was ponder the question and hope that someday, we could all find the peace and contentment that Edwin had found.

According to a recent American Psychological Association (APA) survey, money is Americans' biggest stress source. The survey found that 72% of adults reported feeling stressed about money at some point during the past month. In addition, 22% of adults reported feeling "extreme stress" about money during the same period.

The survey also revealed that financial stress is impacting people's physical health. For example, 33% of adults reported skipping a doctor's appointment or postponing medical treatment because of financial concerns. Furthermore, 51% of adults said that they had experienced at least one symptom of stress, such as headaches, fatigue, or difficulty sleeping, in the past month.

When asked about the causes of their financial stress, the survey found that the top sources were:

1. Paying for essentials like housing, food, and healthcare (64%)
2. Saving for retirement (49%)
3. Paying off debt (42%)
4. Paying for children's education (29%)
5. Unexpected expenses like car repairs or medical bills (29%)

The survey also found that financial stress impacted different demographic groups differently.

For example, 77% of women reported feeling stressed about money compared to 67% of men. In addition, 80% of adults aged 18-29 reported feeling stressed about money, compared to 64% of adults aged 72 or older.

In another recent survey conducted by Wealth-X, a global wealth intelligence and prospecting company, many millionaires felt like they didn't have enough money, even though they were already wealthy. In the survey, Wealth-X interviewed 500 millionaires from around the world and found that:

- 62% of millionaires said they did not consider themselves wealthy
- 22% of millionaires said they would need to accumulate 2-3 times their current wealth to consider themselves wealthy
- 8% of millionaires said they would need 4-5 times their current wealth to consider themselves wealthy

When asked why they didn't feel wealthy, many millionaires cited concerns about maintaining their lifestyle, supporting their families, and ensuring their financial security. They also expressed anxiety about economic volatility, market fluctuations, and the possibility of losing their wealth.

In addition, many of the millionaires interviewed revealed that they always strive for more, even though they already have significant wealth. When asked how much money would be enough, many responded with "a little bit more." Some even said they didn't have a specific number in mind and would continue accumulating wealth as long as possible.

The survey shows that the desire for more money and financial security is a common concern even among the world's wealthiest individuals. While some millionaires may have already accumulated vast wealth, they still need to accumulate more to maintain their lifestyles and ensure their future financial security.

Money has become so integral to our lives that we often forget its true nature. We view it as a means to an end, a way to acquire things we want and need. But in reality, money is nothing more than a tool, an instrument of exchange that allows us to receive goods and services. It is not a measure of our worth or an indicator of our happiness.

Yet, despite this, many of us find ourselves obsessing over money. We need more about being able to pay our bills and maintain our lifestyles. We measure our success by our bank accounts and our possessions. More money will bring us happiness and fulfillment.

But in reality, this obsession with money only leads to more stress, anxiety, and dissatisfaction. We become trapped in a cycle of always wanting more and never being satisfied with what we have. We forget that true contentment comes not from material possessions but from within.

The philosopher Epictetus once said, "Wealth consists not in having great possessions, but in having few wants." This is a profound truth that we would do well to remember. It is not the accumulation of wealth that brings happiness but the contentment that comes from satisfaction with what we have.

We must learn to be content with enough to break free from the cycle of always wanting more. We must shift our focus away from material possessions and toward the things that truly matter - our relationships, passions, and a sense of purpose.

This is not to say that money is unimportant. We need money to survive, to provide for ourselves and our families. But we must remember that it is only a means to an end. We must use it wisely and with purpose rather than allowing it to control us.

Wesley Snipes was at the height of his career in Hollywood. He was a successful actor known for his leading roles in blockbuster hits like "Blade" and "White Men Can't Jump." He had fame, fortune, and a lavish lifestyle that most people could only dream of.

But despite his success, Snipes became increasingly obsessed with chasing more money. He began investing in several high-risk ventures, hoping to increase his wealth further. One of these ventures was a tax shelter scheme that promised to reduce his taxes by millions.

Snipes believed these investments would bring him even greater wealth and success, but he soon learned they were less lucrative than he had hoped. They were downright fraudulent.

In 2008, Snipes was convicted of three counts of willful failure to file income tax returns for 1999, 2000, and 2001. He was sentenced to three years and ordered to pay $17 million in back taxes, penalties, and interest.

It was a stunning fall from grace for the once-successful actor. Snipes' obsession with money and desire for even greater wealth led him down a dangerous path. His greed had clouded his judgment, and he had become blind to the risks and dangers of his investments.

In the end, Snipes paid a heavy price for his actions. He lost his freedom, his reputation, and a significant amount of his wealth. His story is a cautionary tale about the dangers of greed and the importance of being content with what we have. For Snipes, the pursuit of more money led to his downfall. But for others, it is a reminder to be grateful for what we have and to focus on the things that truly matter.

Jordan Belfort had it all - money, power, and prestige. As a Wall Street trader in the late 1980s, he was at the top of his game. He made millions of dollars a year, lived in a luxurious mansion, and spent his days surrounded by beautiful women and fast cars.

But for Belfort, it was never enough. He became obsessed with the idea of making even more money, of achieving even greater success. He and his colleagues engaged in several illegal activities, including insider trading, money laundering, and securities fraud. They defrauded their clients with millions of dollars while living a life of excess and indulgence.

Belfort's greed and corruption eventually caught up with him. In 1998, he was arrested and charged with multiple fraud and money laundering counts. He was sentenced to four years and ordered to pay his victims back $110 million in restitution.

As Belfort sat in his prison cell, he had plenty of time to reflect on his life and actions. He realized that his obsession with money had led him down a dangerous path, one that had caused untold harm to others and ultimately led to his downfall.

It was a harsh lesson but one that Belfort took to heart. After his release from prison, he turned his life around and began speaking out against the dangers of greed and corruption in the financial industry. He wrote a memoir, "The Wolf of Wall Street," which was later turned into a movie starring Leonardo DiCaprio.

Belfort's story is a cautionary tale about the dangers of greed and the consequences of pursuing wealth at all costs. It shows that no amount of money or success is worth sacrificing one's integrity or morals. Belfort learned this lesson the hard way, but he has since used his experience to help others avoid making the same mistakes.

David had always been ambitious. He had big dreams and was willing to work hard to achieve them. And for many years, he was successful. He climbed the corporate ladder, earned a comfortable salary, and enjoyed the trappings of success - a big house, a fancy car, and exotic vacations.

But despite all of this success, David was never satisfied. He was always looking for more money, possessions, and status. He compared himself to others, always trying to keep up with the Joneses. He believed he would finally be happy and fulfilled if he had just had what they had.

But this constant pursuit of more came at a cost. David was stressed, anxious, and unhappy. He constantly worried about his finances, always trying to earn and accumulate more. He was never content with what he had, always looking for the next big thing.

It wasn't until David had a wake-up call that he realized the error of his ways. He was diagnosed with a severe illness that threatened his life and forced him to re-evaluate his priorities. He realized that he had been chasing the wrong things and that true happiness and fulfillment were not found in material possessions.

David learned that the hardest financial skill is not about acquiring more but learning to be content with enough. He learned that social comparison is a dangerous game that can never truly satisfy us. He learned that enough is not too little and that true wealth lies not in our possessions but our hearts and minds.

And he learned that many things in life are never worth risking, no matter how significant the potential gain is. Our integrity, values, and relationships are all things we should hold dear and never compromise.

According to Aristotle, the secret of happiness is not found in seeking more but in developing the capacity to enjoy less. He believed that true contentment and fulfillment could not be found in accumulating material possessions but rather in cultivating an appreciation for the simple things in life.

For Aristotle, pursuing more was a dangerous game that could never truly satisfy us. Instead, he urged his followers to focus on developing inner strength, resilience, and wisdom. He believed that by cultivating these qualities, we could learn to be content with what we have and find joy and fulfillment in the present moment.

Aristotle's insights into the human psyche continue to resonate with people today. His emphasis on the importance of inner strength, resilience, and wisdom serves as a reminder that true happiness and fulfillment come not from material possessions but from within. His quote about the capacity to enjoy less is a powerful reminder that enough is truly enough and that pursuing more can lead us to perpetual dissatisfaction and discontent.

Chapter 6: Start Investing As Early As You Can

Two friends, Steven Smith, and Joe Young, grew up together in the same town. Steven was always interested in personal finance and investing, while Joe paid little attention.

At the age of 20, Steven decided to start investing his savings of $10,000 in a diversified portfolio with an average annual return of 7%. Even though he was beginning, he knew the power of compound interest and understood that time was on his side. He was consistent in his approach and invested a portion of his income into his portfolio yearly.

On the other hand, Joe only bothered to learn about investing once he turned 35. He had always thought that investing was too complicated and risky. When he finally decided to invest, he put $50,000 into a portfolio with an average annual return of 7%.

Fast forward to their retirement age, Steven was 65 years old and had been investing for 45 years. Thanks to his early start and consistent investing, his $10,000 had grown to an impressive $239,373.54 due to compound interest.

On the other hand, Joe started investing later, so he only had 30 years of investment experience. Even though he supported a larger sum of money, his portfolio only grew to $226,218.79 due to the shorter investment horizon.

The story of Steven and Joe clearly illustrates the importance of investing as early as possible. Steven's small investment became a sizable nest egg due to the power of compound interest and his long investment horizon. On the other hand, Joe started investing later in life and needed to catch up due to the shorter investment horizon.

Warren Buffett, one of the world's most successful investors, has a famous quote that goes, "Rule #1: Never lose money. Rule #2: Remember rule number 1." This quote has become a cornerstone of his investment philosophy and a guiding principle for many investors.

At first glance, this quote could be more complex. After all, investing involves taking risks, and there are no guarantees in the stock market. However, Buffett's idea of never losing money is not about avoiding all risks or never experiencing a negative return. Instead, it's about minimizing your risk of significant losses and preserving your capital.

Buffett's approach to investing focuses on high-quality companies with a strong track record of profitability, a durable competitive advantage, and a capable management team. By investing in these companies, he reduces his risk of significant losses and increases his chances of long-term success.

In addition to investing in high-quality companies, Buffett emphasizes the importance of patience and discipline. He avoids getting caught up in short-term market fluctuations or hype around smart investments and instead focuses on the fundamentals of the businesses he invests in.

Buffett has generated impressive returns for himself and his investors by following these principles. His approach is not about taking huge risks or making quick profits but building a solid foundation for long-term success.

So why is the idea of never losing money so important? It's because losses are much harder to recover from than gains. For example, if you lose 50% of your portfolio, you must make a 100% return to break even. This means that preserving your capital is crucial for long-term success.

Let's illustrate Buffet's idea by using the following example.

Let's look at two investment scenarios with an average return of 7% over ten years. The first scenario involves a stable investment that consistently returns an average of 7% per year with a maximum negative return of -3% in any given year. The second scenario involves a more volatile investment with returns ranging from +20% to -18% yearly.

In the first scenario, if you invest $10,000 at the beginning of year one, you would have $19,671.02 at the end of year 10. Here's how the returns would look like each year:

Year 1: +7% Year 2: +7% Year 3: +7% Year 4: +7% Year 5: +7% Year 6: +7% Year 7: +7% Year 8: +7% Year 9: +7% Year 10: -3%

As you can see, the returns are consistent and stable with no significant fluctuations. The portfolio experiences a small negative return in year 10, but the overall portfolio is still worth significantly more than the initial investment.

In the second scenario, the result is quite different if you invest the same $10,000 at the beginning of year one in a more volatile investment that returns an average of 7% per year but has high fluctuations. Here are the returns for each year:

Year 1: +20% Year 2: -10% Year 3: +18% Year 4: -8% Year 5: +15% Year 6: -18% Year 7: +12% Year 8: +10% Year 9: -15% Year 10: +5%

As you can see, there are large fluctuations in returns from year to year. Although the average return is the same as the first scenario, the portfolio is worth less at the end of 10 years. The portfolio is only worth $13,711.47, significantly less than the portfolio in the first scenario.

We should consider some criteria before picking stocks that provide stable and consistent returns over time.

Here are seven critical criteria for selecting valuable large-cap domestic stocks:

1. Financial strength: One of the most important criteria for selecting a valuable company is financial strength. Look for companies with a strong balance sheet, high cash reserves, and manageable debt levels. Companies with healthy financials are better equipped to weather economic downturns and have a greater chance of long-term success.

2. Longevity and stability: Companies that have been in business for a long time and have a stable track record of growth and profitability are often suitable investments. These companies have established a strong brand and loyal customer base and have weathered numerous economic cycles.

3. Competitive advantage: A competitive advantage, or moat, sets a company apart. Look for companies with a durable competitive advantage, such as a strong brand, patents, or proprietary technology.

4. Management quality: A company's management team can significantly impact its

success. Look for companies with experienced, capable, and transparent management teams that prioritize long-term growth over short-term gains.

5. Dividend history: Companies with a history of paying dividends are often more stable and mature. Look for companies with a strong track record of delivering and increasing dividends over time.

6. Valuation: Even the best companies can be overpriced. Look for companies with a reasonable valuation relative to their peers and historical valuations.

7. Industry trends: Consider the broader trends impacting the company's industry. Look for companies that are well-positioned to benefit from these trends.

Some examples of large-cap domestic stocks that meet these criteria include:

1. Apple Inc. (AAPL)
2. Johnson & Johnson (JNJ)
3. Visa Inc. (V)
4. Procter & Gamble Co. (PG)
5. Coca-Cola Co. (KO)
6. McDonald's Corporation (MCD)
7. Walmart Inc. (WMT)

These companies have a long history of profitability, strong financials, and a competitive advantage in their respective industries. They also have a track record of paying dividends and are well-positioned to benefit from industry trends.

Warren Buffett is one of the most successful investors in the world, and his investments show how he thinks about money. His portfolio is made up of a number of large-cap domestic stocks that he chose carefully based on several factors.

Buffett's focus on financially strong companies is reflected in his investment in Bank of America. When the company was trading at a significant discount to its book value, he saw an opportunity to invest in a company with strong fundamentals and a solid balance sheet.

In addition, Buffett's portfolio includes companies that have been around for decades, such as Coca-Cola and Johnson & Johnson. These companies have established a strong brand and a loyal customer base, which reflects Buffett's focus on longevity and stability.

Buffett's investment in Apple, one of his largest holdings, also aligns with his investment philosophy. Apple has a durable competitive advantage, a dominant position in the smartphone market, and a robust ecosystem of products and services. This aligns with Buffett's focus on investing in companies with a competitive advantage.

Buffett's portfolio reflects his focus on valuation. For example, his investment in American Express was made when the company was trading at a discount to its historical valuation. Buffett has generated impressive returns over the years by focusing on undervalued companies.

Warren Buffett's investment holdings demonstrate his investment philosophy of investing in financially strong companies with a durable competitive advantage, a long history of profitability, and a reasonable valuation. This approach has proven successful for Buffett and is a reminder that a disciplined and patient investment strategy can lead to long-term success in the stock market.

Many people feel intimidated by the idea of investing in the stock market. They may need a deep understanding of financial statements and stock analysis to make informed investment decisions. However, many low-cost ETFs provide access to high-quality companies without requiring extensive research or study.

ETFs, or exchange-traded funds, are investment funds that allow investors to buy a diversified portfolio of stocks or other assets. This provides investors with exposure to a broad range of companies and reduces their risk of losses from a single stock. Here are some examples of ETFs that invest in high-quality stocks:

1. Vanguard Total Stock Market ETF (VTI): This ETF tracks the performance of the entire U.S. stock market, providing exposure to companies of all sizes and across all sectors. Its historical return over the past decade is around 14% annually.

2. iShares S&P 500 ETF (IVV): This ETF tracks the performance of the S&P 500 index, which includes 500 of the largest and most well-established U.S. companies. Its historical return over the past decade is around 15% annually.

3. Invesco QQQ ETF (QQQ): This ETF tracks the performance of the Nasdaq 100 index, which includes 100 of the largest non-financial companies listed on the Nasdaq exchange. Its historical return over the past decade is around 21% annually.

These ETFs are just a few examples of the many options available to investors. They provide exposure to high-quality companies across various sectors, reducing the risk of losses from a single stock.

Investing in these ETFs is also easy and accessible for ordinary people. Many online brokerages, such as Robinhood, TD Ameritrade, and E-Trade, offer the ability to buy and sell ETFs with low fees and no minimum investment requirements. This makes it possible for even small investors to build a diversified portfolio and benefit from the long-term growth potential of the stock market.

Many believe they can outsmart the market by timing their buys and sells to exploit short-term fluctuations. However, trying to time the market is risky and often unsuccessful. The most reasonable investment strategy for most people is to buy and hold for the long term and practice dollar cost averaging.

Dollar-cost averaging is a strategy where investors invest a fixed amount of money at regular intervals, regardless of the current market conditions. This strategy helps to reduce the risk of investing a large sum of money all at once when the market is high and also takes advantage of lower prices when the market is down.

Consider a hypothetical example to demonstrate the benefits of dollar cost averaging. Suppose an investor has $10,000 and decides to invest it all at once or practice dollar cost averaging over 12 months. Let's assume that the market is volatile, and the value of the investment can fluctuate by as much as 20% over the year.

If the investor invests the full $10,000 at once and the market drops by 20% in the first month, their investment would be worth $8,000. If the market then recovers and rises by 20% over the next 11 months, the investor's investment would be worth $9,600, resulting in a loss of $400.

On the other hand, if the investor practices dollar cost averaging and invests $833.33 each month for 12 months, their investment will average over time. If the market drops by 20% in the first month, the investor's investment would only be worth $666.67. However, if the market recovers and rises by 20% over the next 11 months, the investor's investment would be worth $9,600, resulting in a gain of $600.

This hypothetical example demonstrates the benefits of dollar cost averaging. By investing a fixed amount at regular intervals, the investor can take advantage of lower prices when the market is down and avoid the risk of investing a large sum of money at a high point in the market.

However, the reality could be more encouraging.

Investing early in life is crucial for financial security, yet many Americans may need to start their investment journey earlier. The Bankrate Financial Security Index Survey conducted in January 2019 aimed to understand the current state of investment habits among American adults and identify potential areas for improvement.

Methodology: YouGov conducted the survey online on behalf of Bankrate.com among 1,010

American adults aged 18 and above. Participants were asked questions about their investment habits, including when they started investing, the types of investments they made, and the reasons for delaying investment.

Results: The survey revealed that most Americans should be investing earlier. Specifically:

- Only 16% of respondents had started investing before the age of 25.
- More than 50% of respondents had begun investing after age 35.
- The largest group of investors (26% of respondents) started investing after age 50.

The survey also found that the main reasons for delaying investment were:

- Not having enough money to invest (32% of respondents)
- Prioritizing other financial obligations (21% of respondents)
- Lack of knowledge or understanding of investing (16% of respondents)
- Fear of losing money (10% of respondents)
- Lack of trust in the stock market or financial institutions (9% of respondents)

The Bankrate Financial Security Index Survey highlights the need for greater financial education and awareness to encourage more Americans to invest early. Delaying investment can have severe consequences for long-term financial security, and the reasons for postponing investment can be overcome with education, resources, and support. By making investing more accessible and approachable, we can help more Americans achieve financial independence and security.

In contrast, another recent survey done by Fidelity Investments aimed to determine what separates self-made millionaires from the rest. They surveyed over 1,100 self-made millionaires across the United States to explore their investment habits, sources of income, and attitudes toward money.

As the survey results came in, a story began to emerge. The majority of self-made millionaires had accumulated their wealth through a combination of investing, saving, and entrepreneurship. Regular investing was identified as a key driver of their financial success, with more than 80% of the respondents attributing their wealth accumulation to consistent investments over the long term.

The most popular investment vehicles among the respondents were stocks, mutual funds, and exchange-traded funds (ETFs). They also reported making regular contributions to their investment portfolios rather than attempting to time the market.

The survey results show that self-made millionaires understand that wealth accumulation takes time and discipline. Following their example, ordinary investors can achieve similar success and build wealth over time. The key is to adopt a long-term mindset, make regular investments, and be patient.

The Fidelity Investments survey offers valuable insight into the millionaire mindset and provides a roadmap for those looking to achieve financial independence and security. With the proper education, resources, and support, anyone can embrace the millionaire mindset and take control of their financial future.

Chapter 7: Luck and Randomness

Richard Branson, the founder of Virgin Group, was born into a well-off family in England in 1950, giving him access to resources and opportunities many others did not have. However, a chance encounter with a young woman at a record store in the 1960s would change his life forever.

Branson and his friend had gone to the store to buy some records, but when they arrived, they found that the store was closing. However, the young woman who worked there was looking to sell off some of the remaining stock, and Branson and his friend saw an opportunity to make some money.

They bought up the remaining stock and sold it out of the trunk of their car, making a profit in the process. This experience gave Branson a taste for entrepreneurship, and he soon began exploring other business opportunities.

In 1970, Branson founded Virgin as a mail-order record company, and it quickly grew into a successful business. However, a lucky break in the music industry catapulted Virgin to success.

In 1973, Branson was trying to sign a band called Tubular Bells to his record label but needed help securing the project's financing. However, a chance encounter with a wealthy Arab sheik on a flight to

London changed everything. Branson initiated a conversation with the sheik, who offered to invest in the project, giving Virgin the funds it needed to produce and release the album.

Tubular Bells became a huge success, and Virgin Records soon became one of the world's most successful and influential record labels. Branson's luck continued to hold as he found several other successful businesses, including Virgin Atlantic Airways and Virgin Mobile.

While Branson's talent, hard work, and entrepreneurial spirit were undoubtedly essential factors in his success, his lucky encounters with the young woman at the record store and the wealthy sheik gave him the opportunities he needed to achieve greatness. Virgin and Branson's other businesses might never have taken off as they did without these chance encounters.

Sara Blakely, the founder of Spanx, was born in Florida in 1971 and worked several odd jobs after college, including as a stand-up comedian and a salesperson for a fax machine company. However, a chance encounter with a pair of ill-fitting white pants would change her life forever.

Blakely was getting ready for a party one night and wanted to wear white pants. However, she found that none of the undergarments she owned were suitable to wear with the pants, as they created visible lines and bumps. She cut the feet off a pair of pantyhose and wore them under the pants instead, which smoothed out her silhouette and gave her a more flattering look.

This experience gave Blakely the idea to create a line of undergarments designed to smooth and shape the body without creating visible lines or discomfort. She spent the next two years researching and developing the product and eventually launched Spanx in 2000.

While Blakely's hard work and determination were essential factors in Spanx's success, she also benefited greatly from a stroke of luck early on in the company's history. Blakely had struggled to secure financing for the company, but a chance encounter with a Neiman Marcus buyer changed everything. Blakely persuaded the buyer to place a large order for Spanx products, giving her the funding she needed to expand the company and take it to the next level.

Today, Spanx is a hugely successful company that generates millions annually. Blakely's idea for a line of comfortable and flattering undergarments has revolutionized the fashion industry. Her story is a testament to the power of luck and determination to achieve success.

Sean Edwards was born in London in 1986 and was the son of Guy Edwards, a former Formula One driver. Sean followed in his father's footsteps and became a professional race car driver, competing in several series worldwide.

However, in 2013, Edwards' life was cut tragically short when he died in a plane crash while conducting a driver coaching session in Australia. He was just 26 years old.

At the time of his death, Edwards was widely regarded as one of the most talented young drivers in the world. He had won numerous championships and secured several high-profile sponsorships, including with Red Bull and Porsche.

Many believed that Edwards had the potential to become a superstar in the world of motorsport. He had already proven himself to be a talented and versatile driver and had attracted the attention of some of the biggest teams in the sport.

However, his premature death meant he could never fulfill his potential. The world of motorsport was deprived of one of its most promising young talents, and Edwards' family and friends were left to mourn the loss of a gifted and passionate individual.

Edwards' story serves as a reminder that business success, as in life, is often determined as much by luck as it is by talent and hard work. Even the most talented individuals can be cut down by unfortunate circumstances, leaving a legacy of unfulfilled potential and unrealized dreams.

One theory that supports the idea that luck plays a significant role in determining success is the "randomness hypothesis," which suggests that chance events play an important role in determining an individual's success or failure.

According to this theory, many factors are outside an individual's control, such as their genetic makeup, the socio-economic conditions they were born into, and the opportunities available. While hard work, talent, and dedication may increase an individual's chances of success, luck still plays a significant role in determining who ultimately achieves success.

Empirical studies have also proved that luck plays a significant role in success. For example, studies have shown that success across individuals often follows a power law distribution, where few individuals achieve disproportionate success. In contrast, most individuals achieve only modest levels of success.

Additionally, research has shown that success often depends on factors outside an individual's control, such as the timing of market opportunities, the location of where an individual was born, and even the weather.

While hard work and talent certainly contribute to an individual's success, luck also significantly determines who ultimately achieves success. The randomness hypothesis provides a valuable framework for understanding why some people achieve great success while others do not and why most people fall somewhere in between.

In light of this theory, it is important to be cautious about whom we praise and admire and whom we look down upon and wish to avoid becoming. Those who have achieved great success may have done so through talent, hard work, and luck. While it is natural to admire and respect their accomplishments, we should also recognize that luck may have played a significant role in their success.

Similarly, those who have not succeeded may have experienced setbacks and failures beyond their control. It is unfair to judge them harshly or dismiss them as lacking talent or drive without considering the role that luck may have played in their lives.

Our perceptions of success and failure should be tempered by an awareness of the role that chance and luck play in our lives. We should strive to be compassionate and empathetic towards others, recognizing that their experiences are shaped by a complex interplay of factors, many of which are beyond their control.

By cultivating a more nuanced and compassionate view of success and failure, we can create a more just and equitable society where everyone is valued and respected, regardless of their achievements or setbacks. We can learn to appreciate the inherent randomness of life and recognize that our successes and failures are not solely the result of our efforts or abilities but also of the unpredictable nature of the universe. In doing so, we can develop a more humble and empathetic approach to life and create a more harmonious and compassionate world.

Social Comparison Theory, proposed by psychologist Leon Festinger in 1954, offers insights into how people evaluate themselves by comparing themselves to others. According to this theory, people tend to compare themselves to others similar in age, gender, occupation, and other relevant factors.

Comparing themselves to others who are more successful or wealthy can lead to negative emotions such as envy, jealousy, and low self-esteem. This can be particularly damaging to one's mental health and well-being. Such negative emotions can also create a sense of inadequacy and anxiety, resulting in depression or other psychological distress.

Moreover, social comparison can also create a fixation on materialistic values and pursuing wealth and success at all costs. This often leads to emptiness, dissatisfaction, and disregard for other important matters, such as compassion, empathy, and social justice.

Therefore, we must know how social comparisons impact our perceptions of ourselves and others. Rather than blindly admiring individuals' wealth and success, it is crucial to adopt a more balanced and compassionate approach to evaluating our worth and the worth of others.

By focusing on the intrinsic value of personal qualities and positive actions rather than on external achievements, we can develop a more positive and self-affirming mindset. We can also learn to appreciate the diversity of human experience and the unique contributions of each individual to the world around us.

One famous economist who attributes a significant portion of investment success to luck is Burton Malkiel. Malkiel is the author of the best-selling book "*A Random Walk Down Wall Street,*" which argues that the market is mainly efficient and that trying to beat it through active management is futile.

Malkiel's famous quote on the role of luck in investment is: "The market is a giant casino, and most people lose." He believes that while skill and knowledge are important in investing, luck plays a significant role in determining investment outcomes.

Malkiel's views on the role of luck in investment are supported by research. Studies have shown that individual investors often underperform the market and that even professional investors struggle to outperform their benchmarks consistently.

Furthermore, the global financial crisis of 2008-2009 highlighted the unpredictable nature of financial markets, with many highly regarded investors and financial institutions suffering significant losses.

Malkiel's view has important implications for investors. Rather than relying on speculation or trying to beat the market through active management, investors should focus on building diversified portfolios that reflect their long-term investment goals and risk tolerance.

It also highlights the importance of adopting a humble and measured approach to investing, which recognizes the limitations of individual knowledge and expertise and emphasizes the importance of long-term planning and risk management.

The SPIVA Scorecard, reported by S&P Dow Jones Indices, tracks the performance of actively managed mutual funds versus their benchmark index over five years. The most recent report covering 2020 found that most active funds underperformed their benchmark index.

For example, the report found that over five years ending in 2020, 74% of large-cap funds underperformed the S&P 500 index. Similarly, 78% of mid-cap funds underperformed the S&P MidCap 400 index, and 82% of small-cap funds underperformed the S&P SmallCap 600 index.

These findings are consistent with other studies showing that professional investors, including mutual fund managers and hedge fund managers, struggle to outperform their benchmarks consistently.

One reason is that active management fees and expenses can erode returns over time, making it more challenging to achieve superior returns. Additionally, the market is highly efficient, with new information and market trends quickly incorporated into stock prices, making it difficult for investors to outperform.

One prominent example of an investment expert who recognizes the role of luck in investment success is John Bogle, the founder of the Vanguard Group and creator of the first index fund.

Bogle has argued that trying to beat the market through active management is a losing game and that investors should focus on low-cost index funds that track the market as a whole. He believes that investors should be cautious of high fees and expenses associated with active management, which can erode returns and make it challenging to achieve superior returns.

Bogle's philosophy is based on the idea that the market is mainly efficient and that trying to beat it through stock picking and active management is often futile. He believes investors should focus on building diversified portfolios aligning with their long-term investment goals and risk tolerance.

His approach has been validated by research, which has consistently shown that active management strategies are unlikely to consistently outperform the market in the long term. Instead, low-cost index funds have been established to provide a reliable and sustainable path to investment success over the long term.

As the sun rose over the bustling city, John walked out of his luxurious apartment with a wide smile. Life had been treating him exceptionally well lately. His investments had paid off, his business was booming, and his bank account was overflowing. But little did he know that this good fortune was less secure than it seemed.

He was reminded of this as he walked down the street, lost in thought. Luck had played a significant role in his success, and he knew it could just as quickly turn against him. He had to acknowledge the cousin of luck - risk. A single wrong decision could erase all his achievements in the blink of an eye.

On the other hand, he had also learned that failure was only sometimes a reliable teacher. It was often easy for smart people to blame themselves for bad outcomes, even when it was beyond their control. The risk was unforgiving, and even the most prudent decisions could lead to failure.

John had found a way to balance this risk by arranging his finances to survive bad investments or missed financial goals. This strategy allowed him to keep playing until the odds fell in his favor.

He knew that success and failure were two sides of the same coin, and it was essential to recognize the role of luck and risk in both. He had learned to forgive himself and understand that nothing was as good or bad as it seemed.

As John pondered his life's ups and downs, he thought of his friend, Tom, who had pushed his luck too far. Tom had always been a risk-taker, which had paid off initially. But eventually, his luck ran out, and he lost everything.

Tom had not planned for failure, and when it came, he was unprepared. His financial life was not arranged so that he could survive a few setbacks, and he had to start from scratch.

John knew that the key to success was taking risks and managing them. Tom had learned this lesson hard, and John was determined to avoid making the same mistake.

The sun was setting, and John walked back into his apartment, grateful for his good fortune and aware of the risk that came with it. He knew he had to stay vigilant and manage his risks carefully, or his luck might run out as quickly as it had come.

Chapter 8: Why Accumulation is Only Half the Battle

Nick Leeson was a young and ambitious trader at Barings Bank, one of Britain's oldest and most respected banks. He had a gift for making speculative trades on the futures market, and his successes quickly earned him a promotion to head up the bank's operations in Singapore.

Leeson's wife, Lisa, had accompanied him to Singapore, excited about the adventure of living abroad. They had met in college, where Lisa had been attracted to Nick's charisma and charm. She was proud of his success and looked forward to their life together.

But as Nick's responsibilities grew, he became increasingly obsessed with making profits. He spent long hours at the office, neglecting his relationship with Lisa. She tried to talk to him about his work, but he would brush her off, telling her that she wouldn't understand the complexities of the market.

One day, Nick's friend and coworker, Andy, dropped by his office. "Hey man, I heard you're doing some pretty crazy trades," he said.

Nick grinned. "Yeah, I'm pushing the limits a bit. But it's paying off. Big time."

Andy raised an eyebrow. "You sure it's worth the risk? What if something goes wrong?"

Nick waved a hand. "I've got it under control. Don't worry about it."

But as the months passed, Nick's bets became riskier and riskier. He began to engage in fraud and forgery, creating a series of fictitious trades and hiding them from the bank's auditors. He was so deep in debt that he felt he had no choice but to continue making increasingly risky trades, hoping to make up for his earlier losses.

Lisa began to notice that something was wrong. Nick was constantly on edge, snapping at her for minor things. She tried to talk to him about it, but he would shut her out.

One night, she confronted him. "Nick, I know something's wrong. You're not yourself anymore. What's going on?"

Nick sighed. "It's just work. It's been stressful lately."

Lisa shook her head. "It's more than that. I can tell. Please, talk to me."

Nick hesitated, then told her about the pressures he was under at work, his accumulated debt, and the lies he had spoken. Lisa was shocked and angry, but she also felt sorry for him. "We'll get through this together," she told him.

But as the Asian financial crisis of 1997 hit, Nick's scheme began to unravel. The markets plummeted, leaving him with massive losses he could not cover. Despite his attempts to hide the truth, the bank eventually discovered his activities and declared bankruptcy.

Nick was arrested and extradited to the UK to face trial. He was ultimately sentenced to six and a half years in prison for his role in the scandal. Lisa was left to pick up the pieces of their shattered life together.

The takeaway from this story is that generating profits is only part of the equation in achieving success in business and investment. Preserving and managing wealth is equally important. The ability to resist impulsive decisions, maintain a long-term focus, and manage risk effectively are crucial to success in these fields.

Preserving wealth involves a deep understanding of financial markets, adaptability to changing conditions, and the ability to make sound decisions amidst uncertainty. This requires discipline, patience, ongoing education, and a commitment to self-improvement.

It also requires a fundamental understanding of the role of money in our lives, the meaning of success, and the nature of human desire. Managing and preserving wealth over the long term involves confronting difficult questions and developing self-awareness and self-control.

The concept of survival is central to achieving success in business and investment. It requires the ability to resist the temptation of short-term gains and focus on the long-term preservation of wealth. Cultivating discipline and self-awareness is key to thriving in this environment.

By focusing on preserving and managing wealth, we can achieve lasting success and fulfillment in our personal and professional lives.

John Paulson, the founder of Paulson & Company, is a hedge fund manager who became famous for his bet against the US housing market in 2007. Paulson's firm made a massive profit by correctly predicting the subprime mortgage crisis and investing heavily in credit default swaps.

Despite this early success, Paulson has emphasized the importance of survival and longevity in finance. In a 2011 interview with Business Insider, he noted that "the most important thing in investment management is survival" and that focusing on risk management and capital preservation is key to long-term success.

By prioritizing survival and longevity, Paulson has built a successful investment firm that has weathered numerous market cycles and economic crises. His focus on risk management and capital preservation has helped him navigate even the most challenging market conditions. His emphasis on long-term thinking has inspired many other investors to follow in his footsteps.

A survey conducted by Spectrem Group, a wealth management research firm, found that most ultra-high-net-worth individuals attributed their success to hard work, smart investing, and careful financial planning. These individuals had built their fortunes through careful planning and disciplined decision-making.

The survey revealed that these affluent individuals were more likely to prioritize saving and investing over spending on luxury goods and services. Rather than indulging in extravagant purchases, nearly three-quarters of respondents preferred to buy products and services that were practical and functional.

The survey also found that ultra-high-net-worth individuals were likelier to invest long-term. They focused on building diversified portfolios and avoided impulsive decisions. More than half of respondents said they worked with a financial advisor to help them achieve their long-term financial goals, and nearly 40% said they had a written financial plan.

Like a sturdy ship built to withstand rough seas and reach its destination safely, my financial plan is designed to make me unbreakable against economic storms and allow me to achieve my long-term goals. Instead of chasing quick riches like a sailor chasing treasure, I prioritize financial stability and resilience like a captain securing their ship's hull and crew before embarking on a long voyage.

In the same way that a sturdy oak tree grows tall and strong by slowly absorbing nutrients from the soil and weathering harsh winds, my investment strategy is built to grow steadily over time and withstand market fluctuations. Rather than trying to reach for the sky like a vine grasping at a trellis, I cultivate patience and discipline like a gardener tending to their crops and waiting for the right time to harvest.

In 1991, the American tech company Compaq had a brilliant plan to launch a new laptop computer called the Compaq LTE. They had spent months preparing for the launch, pouring millions of dollars into research, development, and marketing.

However, just a few days before the launch was set to take place, Hurricane Bob struck the northeastern United States, causing widespread damage and power outages. This threatened to derail Compaq's launch, as stores and distribution centers were closed, and customers could not access the internet to learn about the new product.

But rather than giving up on their plans, Compaq's leadership team quickly sprang into action, putting their contingency plans into effect. They shifted their marketing strategy to focus on print and radio ads instead of online campaigns. They worked with their distributors to find alternative ways to get the laptops into stores.

As a result of their quick thinking and planning, Compaq was able to salvage the launch and achieve record-breaking sales for the Compaq LTE. By planning for the plan not going according to plan, they were able to weather the unexpected storm and come out even stronger on the other side.

While planning is crucial to any successful endeavor, preparing for the unexpected and planning contingencies are equally important. The most important part of any plan is not just the plan itself but the ability to adapt and adjust when things don't go as expected.

Effective planning is like charting a course for a long journey. Just as a sailor sets a system based on the prevailing winds and tides, a well-designed plan considers a range of variables and factors.

However, just as the weather can change unexpectedly and alter a ship's course, plans can also be disrupted by unexpected challenges and circumstances. The essential part of any plan is not just the plan itself but the ability to navigate rough seas and adjust course as needed.

This requires a mindset of flexibility and adaptability, like a captain who must be prepared to adjust course on the fly in response to changing conditions. By building in contingencies and preparing for the unexpected, we can steer our plans through stormy waters and emerge stronger on the other side.

It is crucial to be simultaneously hopeful about the future and cautious about the risks and challenges ahead. It requires a balanced mindset to anticipate and prepare for potential roadblocks while remaining optimistic about long-term goals and aspirations.

It is like a tightrope. It requires a delicate balance between confidence and caution, courage and prudence. By staying focused on the end goal while remaining alert to potential pitfalls, we can chart a course toward success and navigate the ups and downs of life with resilience and determination.

It is also like a mountaineer climbing a treacherous peak. It requires a delicate balance between optimism, paranoia, courage, and caution to reach the summit and conquer the mountain.

On the one hand, optimism is like the mountaineer's belief in overcoming any obstacle and reaching the peak. It gives them the motivation and courage to take on the challenges ahead and the confidence to keep climbing even when the going gets tough.

On the other hand, paranoia is like the mountaineer's awareness of the risks and hazards of climbing a treacherous peak. It keeps them alert to potential dangers and allows them to take precautions and make smart decisions to stay safe.

By balancing these two forces, the mountaineer can climb the peak with confidence and resilience. They can stay focused on their ultimate goal while remaining aware of the risks and challenges and adjust their approach to overcome obstacles.

In 1953, Sir Edmund Hillary and Tenzing Norgay set out to become the first climbers to reach Mount Everest's summit, the world's highest peak. The journey would take them through treacherous terrain, high altitudes, and unpredictable weather conditions.

As they began their ascent, Hillary and Norgay embodied a barbell personality, balancing optimism about their goal with a healthy paranoia about the dangers ahead. They were determined to reach the summit but aware of the risks and hazards that could threaten their journey.

Hillary and Norgay encountered numerous obstacles and setbacks throughout their climb, from icy terrain to avalanches and fierce winds. But they remained focused on their ultimate goal and adjusted their approach to stay safe and navigate the challenges.

Finally, on May 29, 1953, after months of preparation and weeks of climbing, Hillary and Norgay reached the summit of Mount Everest, becoming the first humans in history to stand at the top of the world.

Their success was due in no small part to their barbell personality, which allowed them to stay focused on their goal while remaining aware of the risks and challenges ahead. By balancing optimism and paranoia, courage, and caution, they achieved a feat many believed was impossible.

In the world of business and life,

The key to success is balance, not strife,

A barbell personality, we must embrace,

Optimism and paranoia in proper space.

Planning is key; that much is clear,

But the plan must be flexible, we must steer,

Through stormy seas and unexpected tides,

Adapting as we go, with careful strides.

Wealth is not just about making a lot,

It's about survival and keeping what we've got,
Frugality, resilience, and a long-term view,

These are the traits that will pull us through.

In life and business, there are no guarantees,

Only the winds of change and the unexpected breeze,
but with a barbell personality and a flexible plan,

We can weather any storm and be a success in our span.

So let us embrace the challenges that come our way, And
navigate the ups and downs of life with grace and play,

With optimism and paranoia, planning and
adaptability, We can achieve our wildest dreams and
make them a reality.

Chapter 9: The Price of Achievement

A small town was nestled in a valley, surrounded by rolling hills and lush green forests. Three best friends lived in this town: Tom, Jerry, and Harry. They were young and ambitious and dreamed of making it big globally.

One day, they stumbled upon a magical fountain in the forest's heart. The fountain was said to grant wishes to anyone who threw a coin. Excited by the prospect of fulfilling their dreams, the three friends decided to try their luck.

Tom wished to become a successful businessman, Jerry wanted to become a famous musician, and Harry wished to become a renowned artist. They threw their coins into the fountain and waited for their wishes to come true.

To their surprise, the fountain started glowing, and a voice boomed, "Your wishes have been granted. But remember, nothing is free; everything has a price."

Excited by their newfound success, the friends set out to achieve their dreams. Tom worked day and night, taking risks, making sacrifices, and facing numerous challenges to establish his business. Jerry spent countless hours practicing his music, performing at small gigs, and overcoming rejection and criticism to become a successful musician. Harry dedicated himself to his art, spending sleepless nights, taking on odd jobs, and facing criticism and refusal to become a renowned artist.

As they achieved their dreams, they realized that the price they had paid was much higher than they had imagined. Tom had sacrificed his family time and dealt with numerous headaches and risks in his business. Jerry had missed many personal events and relationships, and Harry struggled with financial difficulties and creative blocks.

But they had no regrets. They knew their hard work and dedication had paid off, and nothing worth having came easy. They had learned that everything comes with a price and that success and happiness are not free.

All things come with a cost, and often the secret to successful financial management is identifying that cost and having the courage to pay it. However, the difficulty lies in the fact that the price of many things is concealed until we are forced to confront it head-on when it's too late to do anything about it.

This dilemma underscores the importance of recognizing the actual cost of our financial decisions before they come due. Before undertaking, we must research the potential costs and risks of investments, savings plans, and financial goals. We must be mindful of the hidden fees associated with loans, credit cards, and other forms of borrowing.

Failure to heed this warning can result in devastating financial consequences that can be difficult to overcome. Late fees, high-interest rates, and mounting debt can quickly spiral out of control, leading to financial ruin and personal distress.

Investing in the stock market can be compared to navigating a stormy sea. While the destination may be clear and promising, the journey is filled with unpredictable waves, choppy waters, and sudden wind gusts. Just like a sailor must be prepared for the challenges of the open sea, investors must be prepared for the volatility and uncertainty of investing in stocks.

While it's true that the stock market generally rises in the long term, it can also experience significant downturns and losses in a short time. Many factors, such as economic conditions, global events, and political changes, can cause these sudden storms. Just like a sailor must be prepared for unexpected weather patterns, investors must be prepared for unforeseen shifts in the market.

But just as a sailor can navigate rough seas with skill and experience, investors can also manage the stock market's volatility with careful research and strategic planning. By diversifying their portfolios, selecting individual stocks carefully, and remaining disciplined in their investment strategies, investors can ride out the storms of volatility and come out ahead in the long term.

However, like a sailor must remain alert during a storm, investors must stay focused and disciplined during market volatility. Panic selling or rash decisions can lead to financial losses, just as steering the ship into the path of a wave can lead to disaster at sea.

Tesla stock has returned over 18,000% from 2010 to 2021, making it one of the most successful growth stocks in recent history. However, the stock traded below its all-time high on 77% of trading days.

Similarly, Amazon stock has returned over 5,000% from 2001 to 2021, making it one of the most successful stocks of the past two decades. But even with that impressive return, the stock has traded below its previous high on 86% of trading days.

These examples demonstrate that the bigger the returns, the higher the volatility price. Successful investing demands a cost that is only sometimes apparent once you've experienced it firsthand. The emotional price of investing, in the form of fear, doubt, and uncertainty, can be just as high as the financial price.

On the other hand, bonds, particularly government bonds, are often seen as low-risk investments with lower potential returns. However, the opposite of the high-volatility stocks previously mentioned, bonds often require little to no pain for investors to gain returns.

For example, the Vanguard Total Bond Market ETF returned 35% from 2010 to 2021, with only occasional periods of volatility. While the returns may not be as high as those of growth stocks, investors can achieve steady gains without emotional cost.

However, this lower risk and lower volatility come with lower potential returns. The adage "no pain, no gain" often holds in investing. While low-risk investments may require little emotional cost, they also need lower potential returns. To achieve higher returns, investors must be willing to pay the volatility and emotional discomfort of investing in higher-risk assets.

Higher volatility does not necessarily mean higher risk in investing. Volatility refers to the magnitude of fluctuations in the value of an investment over time. While volatile assets may require a higher price, that price does not always translate to higher risk.

Risk refers to the potential for loss. Investing in companies that lose significant amounts of money or go bankrupt is a higher-risk proposition than investing in volatile assets. As Warren Buffett, one of the most successful investors in history, has said, his first rule of investing is not to lose money.

However, even Buffett's biggest holding, Apple, has been volatile in the past. For example, in 2018, Apple's stock price fell more than 30% from its peak. Despite this volatility, Buffett has continued to hold the stock and since rebounded.

Warren Buffett's Berkshire Hathaway holds several other well-known stocks besides Apple, some of which have also experienced volatility.

One example is Coca-Cola, which Berkshire Hathaway has held for decades. While Coca-Cola is often seen as a steady, reliable investment, it has also experienced volatility. In 2020, for example, Coca-Cola's stock price fell nearly 30% from its peak in February before recovering later in the year.

Another example is American Express, another long-time holding of Berkshire Hathaway. American Express has also experienced volatility in the past. In 2016, the company's stock price fell more than 20% after it lost a significant partnership with Costco. However, the stock has since rebounded and performed well overall.

Berkshire Hathaway also holds shares of Goldman Sachs, a prominent investment bank. Like other financial stocks, Goldman Sachs has been subject to volatility. In 2018, the stock price fell nearly 35% from its peak in March before recovering later.

Loss aversion is the idea that people tend to feel the pain of losses more strongly than the pleasure of gains. This can lead to irrational decision-making when it comes to investing, as people may sell their stocks in a panic during periods of market volatility rather than holding on and waiting for the market to rebound.

To overcome loss aversion, investors can focus on the long-term potential of their investments and avoid making impulsive decisions based on short-term market movements. By taking a disciplined and patient approach to investing, investors can stay committed to their investment strategy and avoid being swayed by emotions during market turbulence.

Investing in big-name, reputable companies can provide a sense of comfort and stability for investors during periods of market volatility. These companies are often household names, and investors may see their logos and products daily, making them feel more connected to their investments.

Selling off investments in a panic can be tempting when markets are down. However, investors can avoid making impulsive decisions based on short-term market movements by holding stocks in reputable companies.

Take Amazon, for example. With a market capitalization of over $1.6 trillion as of March 2023, Amazon is a giant in the world of e-commerce. The company's name and logo are recognizable worldwide, and its products and services are used by millions daily. By investing in Amazon, investors can benefit from the stability and familiarity of a well-known brand.

Another example is Microsoft, with a market capitalization of over $2.3 trillion as of March 2023. Microsoft is a software and cloud computing leader with diverse products and services spanning multiple industries. The company's stability and strong track record of success can reassure investors during market turbulence.

Another helpful psychological approach is called framing. "Framing is the idea that how we think about a decision can impact our feelings." In investing, framing can help investors reframe market downturns as opportunities rather than threats. By viewing market downturns as opportunities to buy quality stocks at a discount, investors can overcome their fear and hold onto their portfolios during periods of market volatility.

Food marketers are experts at framing their products in a way that appeals to consumers. Take candy bars, for example. A company might market its candy bar as "90% fat-free" instead of "10% fat" to make it seem healthier. By framing the product this way, consumers are more likely to buy it, even if it is not a healthy choice.

A study conducted by researchers at Cornell University highlights the power of framing in the food industry. The researchers presented two groups of participants with the same salad but described it in two different ways. The first group was told that the salad was a "diet" salad, while the second group was told that the salad was a "hearty" salad. Despite being presented with the same salad, the participants who were told it was a "hearty" salad consumed significantly more than those who were told it was a "diet" salad.

This study illustrates the importance of being mindful of how information is framed. When making decisions, we must be aware of the potential biases that may be present and consider the context in which the information is presented. By doing so, we can make more informed decisions and avoid being swayed by emotional or irrational factors.

Investing in success can be elusive, and many people need help to come to grips with the true cost of achieving it. When we buy a car, a house, or a vacation, we know exactly what we're getting into. We see the price tag, and we're willing to pay it. But when investing, the price of success is only sometimes immediately apparent. It's like an invisible fee, lurking just below the surface, waiting to pounce when we least expect it.

Many people need help to stick with their investments when the market turns south. They view any loss as a fine, a punishment for doing something wrong. Fines are supposed to be avoided, not embraced. Traffic tickets and IRS penalties mean we've done something wrong and must be punished. It's no wonder that when people see their investments decline, they want to avoid future fines at all costs.

But what if we could change our perspective? What if we could see market volatility as a fee rather than a fine? Think of it like a chef creating a gourmet meal. The chef knows the journey will be long and complex, with many obstacles and challenges. But they also know that staying focused and persevering is essential to creating a masterpiece. When the cooking becomes difficult, and the flavors don't quite come together, it can be tempting to give up or start over. But the chef knows that the price of success is staying the course, no matter what.

Investing is no different. Investors must be prepared for complex challenges and unexpected setbacks, like a chef creating a gourmet meal. But staying focused and persevering is essential to achieving investing success. When markets become volatile, selling off our investments and retreating to the safer ground can be tempting. But like a chef, we must stay focused on our end goal and remember that the price of success is staying the course, no matter what.

It's not always easy, and few investors have the disposition to say, "I'm actually fine if I lose 30% of my money." But if we can shift our mindset and see volatility as a natural part of the investing process, we'll be better equipped to weather the storms and come out ahead.

Chapter 10: Freedom and Happiness

In the land of opportunity, the United States lived a people who seemed to have it all - from massive mansions to fast cars and high-end technology. But despite the abundance of wealth, something was amiss. Happiness was nowhere to be found.

To investigate this, a survey was conducted across multiple countries. The United States ranked only 19th on the World Happiness Report, despite having the highest GDP globally. According to the report, countries like Finland, Denmark, Iceland, Switzerland, and Norway were happier.

Further research revealed the reasons behind this disparity. Income inequality in the US was one of the significant contributors. While the country is indeed wealthy, the wealth is unevenly distributed. The top 1% of Americans own more wealth than the bottom 50%, resulting in financial struggles for many.

The US also has fewer vacation days, less job security, and longer working hours, which can cause stress, burnout, and unhappiness. Americans work an average of 1,780 hours per year, 200 more than the UK and 500 more than France. On top of that, only 54% of Americans use all their vacation days, according to a survey by Glassdoor.

Furthermore, Americans are less likely to have strong social support networks than people in other countries. According to a survey by Cigna, almost half of Americans reported feeling lonely, and over 40% reported feeling isolated. This can severely impact mental health, leading to depression and anxiety.

Countries like Finland, Denmark, Iceland, Switzerland, and Norway ranked higher on the happiness index due to their emphasis on work-life balance, social welfare systems, and freedom. These countries offer universal healthcare, free education, flexible working hours, paid parental leave, and guaranteed vacation days. They also have a higher sense of community, which promotes happiness and well-being.

It's like the US is a luxurious yacht with all the bells and whistles, but it's sailing through turbulent waters. The vessel may have all the amenities of comfort, but the unstable environment keeps everyone on edge and uneasy.

An experiment conducted to explore the relationship between money and happiness is the "Can Money Buy Happiness?" study by Elizabeth Dunn, Lara Aknin, and Michael Norton, published in 2008.

To conduct their experiment, the researchers recruited a group of participants. They randomly assigned them to two groups: one instructed them to spend money on themselves, and another instructed them to spend it on someone else. The participants were given either $5 or $20 to spend and were told to spend the money by the end of the day.

As the sun set on that day, the researchers collected the results. The participants who spent the money on someone else reported a significant increase in happiness. In contrast, those who paid the money themselves did not experience a significant increase, even if they spent a larger amount. It was as if the act of giving had generated a wave of positive emotions, while the front of receiving had left the participants feeling empty and unfulfilled.

The researchers likened the results to a forest. Imagine a forest where the trees are money, and the birds are happy. The birds flutter around, chirping and singing, but never land on the trees. The trees stand tall and proud, but they do not bring happiness. However, when someone plants a seed and tends to it with care, a tree grows, and the birds come flocking. The tree provides a home for the birds, bringing joy and happiness to the forest.

The study concluded that spending money on others can lead to greater happiness than spending money on oneself. The researchers suggested that this effect may be due to the social connections and positive emotions generated when people give to others.

In a world where money reigns supreme, people yearn for the highest form of wealth - waking up each day and saying, “I can do whatever I want today.” They chase riches, believing them to be the key to happiness. But the true treasure lies not in hoards of gold but in the freedom to chart their course.

The desire for liberation often drives the pursuit of wealth. It is the chance to roam the world, own whatever catches their fancy, and live on their terms. Happiness is an elusive concept, yet one thing that unites us all is the need for control. The power to do as we please, when we please, with whomever we please, for as long as we please - that is the ultimate prize. It is the highest dividend money can offer.

For some, wealth is the gateway to a life of abundance. It is the key to open doors that were previously closed. But true happiness cannot be bought. It is a state of mind cultivated through the freedom to pursue one's passions, connect with others, and make a difference in the world.

Like a bird soaring in the sky, true happiness comes from the ability to fly free. To explore the vast expanse of the world without any boundaries. To live life unencumbered by the shackles of financial worry.

It is a gift that cannot be measured in dollars and cents but rather in the quality of one's life.

The pursuit of wealth should be viewed not as an end in itself but as a means to an end - the end being the ability to live a life of our own making. Life is defined by our experiences, the people we meet, and the impact we make. It is a vibrant life in every sense of the word.

Life is a delicate balancing act between time, money, and independence. Money is an essential tool that enables us to have control over our time, allowing us to live a life that is truly our own.

Acquiring financial security in increments is essential for gaining autonomy and freedom over time. It starts with taking a few days off work when sick without fear of financial ruin. It means waiting for the right job to come along instead of taking the first one that comes along, a decision that can be life-changing. It's the ability to remain unafraid of one's employer, knowing that six months of emergency expenses can cushion losing one's job. And finally, financial security means having the freedom to take a job that pays less but offers flexible hours or a shorter commute.

Money is like the brush with which we paint our life's canvas. With every financial decision we make, we add another brushstroke, shaping the masterpiece that is our life. It's an expression of our values, our dreams, and our aspirations for the future.

We must recognize the power of money to grant us control over our time, our resources, and our lives. The ability to create a life that aligns with our vision of the future is a priceless gift that requires careful stewardship of our financial resources

In a world where time is our most precious asset, the ability to control it is the ultimate reward. It allows us to pursue our passions, create meaningful connections with others, and make a difference in the world. So let us use our financial resources wisely, investing in creating a life that is truly our own.

Tony Hsieh was a man who had it all. He was the CEO of Zappos, an online shoe and clothing retailer that had made him millions of dollars. He was a successful entrepreneur who had worked hard to achieve his dreams, but he realized that something was missing.

In an interview with Inc. magazine, Hsieh talked about his journey to happiness. He revealed that he had spent most of his life working long hours, chasing after success and money. He believed money was the key to happiness, but as he got older, he realized there was more to life than work.

Hsieh knew that he needed to make a change. He decided to step down as CEO of Zappos and start investing his time and energy in other areas of his life. He began to focus on his relationships with friends and family, and he started pursuing hobbies that he enjoyed, such as playing video games and attending music festivals.

Hsieh's philosophy was simple - happiness came from having control over your life and your time. He realized that money was just a means to an end and that true happiness came from living a fulfilling and meaningful life.

Sadly, Hsieh passed away in 2020, but his legacy lives on. He showed us that success and happiness are different and that pursuing money can sometimes lead us astray. Instead, he taught us to focus on what truly matters, such as our relationships and passions.

David Kim had always dreamed of making a living from his music, but for years he had to work as a waiter at a restaurant in Los Angeles to pay the bills. Despite the financial strain, David never quit his passion for songwriting and performing.

One day, David's music caught the attention of a record producer named Emma Stevens. She was immediately impressed by his talent and offered him a record deal. David's music soon skyrocketed in popularity, and he found himself making over a million dollars a year.

Despite his newfound wealth, David remained grounded and focused on his music. He knew that money couldn't buy happiness and that his true fulfillment came from doing what he loved. David's life hadn't changed much at all. He still lived in the same small apartment and drove the same old car.

One evening, David was hanging out with his friends at a local bar, including his childhood friend Tim Johnson and his girlfriend, Rachel Rodriguez. David's success amazed Tim and Rachel, and they asked him how his life had changed since he started making so much money.

David laughed and took a sip of his beer. "Honestly, not much has changed," he said. "I'm still the same guy who used to work as a waiter. The extra money is nice, but it's just a number to me. What matters is that I can do what I love every day."

Tim nodded in agreement. "That's awesome, man," he said. "I remember when you used to play gigs at local bars just for a few bucks. Now look at you, making a fortune from your music."

Rachel chimed in, "So, what are you going to do with all that money?"

David shrugged. "I don't know. Maybe save some for a rainy day or donate to some charities I care about. But honestly, I don't need much to be happy. As long as I can keep making music, I'm good."

David's story is a testament to the power of following one's passion and staying true to oneself, even in adversity. In a society that often values financial success above all else, his decision to pursue his love for music, despite its uncertain prospects, is a reminder that there is more to life than just money.

It is also a reminder that happiness and fulfillment come from within, not external circumstances. Despite his financial struggles, David remained focused on his music, knowing it was his true calling. He understood that money was just a means to an end and that true wealth came from doing what he loved.

David's journey can be seen as a metaphor for life itself. We all face challenges and setbacks, but how we respond to those challenges ultimately defines us. Like David, we must stay true to ourselves, follow our passions, and never lose sight of what truly matters.

His story is a reminder that success and happiness are not the same things. While David's financial success was undoubtedly a factor in his happiness, it was not the only one. His true happiness came from doing what he loved and being able to share his music with others. We can all learn from this lesson, no matter our goals or aspirations.

A groundbreaking study published in Social Psychological and Personality Science sought to explore the complex relationship between money and happiness. The study surveyed over 4,000 adults in the United States, asking them about their income, happiness levels, and overall life experiences.

The results were surprising. The researchers found that, on average, individuals who reported having more money did not necessarily report being happier. The study found that more money did not lead to greater happiness once people reached a certain income level.

But what did make people happy? The study found that personal relationships, community involvement, and meaningful work were more strongly associated with happiness than income or wealth.

People with strong social connections and a sense of purpose were much more likely to report feeling happy and fulfilled, regardless of their income level.

This study challenges the common belief that money is the key to happiness. While money is essential for meeting basic needs like food, shelter, and healthcare, it is not the most crucial factor in determining happiness and well-being. The study suggests that pursuing social connections, personal growth, and meaningful pursuits is even more important for our happiness and well-being.

Chapter 11: Passive Incomes with Prices

John Carter is a hardworking man in his early thirties who dreams of financial freedom. John works as a software engineer, saving diligently for years to achieve his goal. But he knows that relying solely on his job to provide for his future is insufficient. John wants to create passive income streams to help him reach his financial goals.

One day, John meets his friend, Judy Thompson, a successful real estate investor. She tells him about the potential for rental income and how it can be a great source of passive income. Intrigued, John decides to buy a rental property and become a landlord. However, he soon realizes that managing a rental property is more active than he had hoped. There are always tenant issues and repairs, and the income could have been more steady than he had expected.

Disappointed but undeterred, John decides to explore other passive income options. He begins to research and learns about other potential income streams, such as being a YouTuber, writing books, and investing in dividend stocks. John is excited about the possibilities and puts energy into creating content and writing his first book.

As John dives deeper into these new endeavors, he realizes they are not 100% passive. Being a YouTuber and writing books require much work, time, and effort to succeed. John starts to feel frustrated and wonders if there truly is such a thing as a completely passive income stream.

At this point, John meets his friend, Steven Kim, a financial advisor specializing in helping people reach their financial goals. Steven listens to John's concerns and shares his experience with passive income streams. He tells John that while they may not be completely passive, they can still be an excellent tool for achieving financial freedom.

Steven explains that passive income streams require a certain amount of work upfront, but once they are established, they can provide a steady source of income that requires minimal effort to maintain. He encourages John to keep pursuing his passive income goals and reminds him that the key is to find something he enjoys that aligns with his skills and interests.

John starts to search for dividend-paying stocks and realizes that while they offer a steady source of income, the yields are sometimes lower than he had hoped. He decides to research and find the best dividend stocks to invest in.

John starts with well-known dividend stocks, such as Coca-Cola and Johnson & Johnson, which have a long history of paying dividends to their shareholders.

He discovers that Coca-Cola yields around 3.1%, while Johnson & Johnson has about 2.5%. While these yields are decent, John must still be satisfied with the returns.

He decides to look for higher-yielding stocks and finds some exciting options. For example, the global real estate company, Simon Property Group, has a dividend yield of 4.69%, while the energy company, Chevron, has a gain of 5.4%. John is excited about these options but hesitates to put all his eggs in one basket.

One day, John is out grabbing lunch with his friend Mike Zheng. As they eat, Mike tells John about a new investment opportunity he recently discovered.

"Hey John, have you ever heard of CEFs?" Mike asks.

John shakes his head. "No, I haven't. What are they?"

"Closed-end funds," Mike explains. "They're a type of investment fund that trades like a stock on an exchange. They can invest in various assets, like stocks, bonds, and real estate, and they can pay out high yields."

John is intrigued. "That sounds interesting. But is it worth the added risk?"

Mike nods. "Well, like any investment, there's always risk involved. But the potential rewards can be great. And if you're looking for a way to generate passive income, CEFs can be a great option."

John starts to get excited about adding CEFs to his portfolio. "Okay, tell me more. How do they work?"

Mike pulls out his phone and starts showing John some examples. "Basically, you buy shares of a CEF just like you would a stock. But the fund is closed-end, meaning a limited number of shares are available. This can create some volatility, but the fund can pay out high yields. And because they invest in a variety of assets, they can help you diversify your portfolio."

John is impressed. "Wow, I had no idea. Do you have any specific CEFs that you recommend?"

Mike nods. "Yeah, there are a few that I like. One is the BlackRock Municipal 2020 Term Trust. It pays out a really high yield and invests in tax-free municipal bonds, which can be a great way to generate passive income without worrying about taxes. There's also the Gabelli Equity Trust, which invests in various stocks and pays out a high yield as well."

John starts to feel more confident about the idea of investing in CEFs. "Thanks for telling me about this, Mike. I'm definitely going to do some more research and consider adding them to my portfolio."

Mike nods. "No problem, man. It's always good to explore different investment opportunities and find ways to generate passive income. I think CEFs could be a great addition to your portfolio and help you reach your financial goals."

Investing in closed-end funds (CEFs) can be a rollercoaster ride of volatility, but the potential rewards of their decent yields make them an excellent tool for generating passive income. CEFs can offer investors a reliable source of income that can be reinvested to grow their portfolio further.

One standout example of a high-yield CEF is the BlackRock Enhanced Equity Dividend Trust (BDJ). This well-diversified fund invests in large-cap companies and rewards investors with a monthly dividend of 6.7%, boasting an impressive yield of 9.18%. The Gabelli Equity Trust (GAB) is another excellent option for investors, with its diverse portfolio spanning several sectors, including technology, healthcare, and financial services. GAB pays a monthly dividend of 6.2%, with a yield of 8.12%.

The high yields that CEFs offer are one of their most attractive features. They provide investors with a steady stream of income that can be used to support their daily lives or reinvested to grow their wealth. In addition, many CEFs are well-diversified, which helps to reduce risk and volatility, providing investors with a smoother ride during turbulent market conditions.

CEFs also offer the potential for capital appreciation, meaning investors can benefit from the underlying assets of the fund growing in value. This potential for growth, combined with the high yields of CEFs, makes them a popular option for income-seeking investors.

One example of a CEF with a long history is the John Hancock Premium Dividend Fund (PDT), launched in 2004. This fund invests primarily in large-cap and mid-cap dividend-paying stocks and has a long history of paying consistent, high-yield dividends to its investors. Its current yield is around 7.7%.

PDT has been paying monthly dividends since its inception, and its investment strategy focuses on companies with a strong track record of dividend growth and sustainability. The fund's portfolio includes well-known companies such as Microsoft, Johnson & Johnson, and Coca-Cola, which have a long history of paying consistent dividends to their shareholders.

Over the years, PDT has demonstrated a strong performance track record and consistently outperformed its benchmark index. However, according to Morningstar, as of March 2023, PDT's standard deviation over the past three years was 20.75%; meanwhile, S&P's standard deviation is around 17%. That means CEFs are generally more volatile than general stock markets. Despite its volatility, PDT has been a popular choice among income-seeking investors looking to generate passive income through dividend investing.

Another example of a CEF with a long history is the John Hancock Preferred Income Fund II (HPF), launched in 1993. This fund invests primarily in preferred stocks and has paid a monthly dividend since inception. Its current yield is around 6.4%.

Another option is the Nuveen Preferred and Income 2022 Term Fund (JPT), which invests in preferred securities and has a termination date of 2022. This fund has been paying a monthly dividend since 2016 and yields around 5.5%.

The Eaton Vance Tax-Advantaged Dividend Income Fund (EVT) is another example of a CEF with a long history. It was launched in 2003 and invested in a mix of dividend-paying stocks and preferred securities. EVT has been paying a monthly dividend since inception, yielding around 7.4%.

Lastly, the PIMCO Corporate & Income Opportunity Fund (PTY), launched in 2002, invests in corporate bonds, mortgage-backed securities, and other fixed-income assets. This fund has been paying a monthly dividend since inception, yielding around 7.6%.

These funds have a long history of paying consistent, high-yield dividends to their investors. While they may be more volatile than other income-generating investments, such as bonds or CDs, they can be a great way to diversify your portfolio and generate passive income over the long term.

After conducting thorough research on CEFs and assessing the risks involved, John concluded that financial freedom and having control over his time were invaluable. He recognized that CEFs were more volatile than the broader stock market, but he was willing to pay this price in exchange for the potential to generate consistent passive income.

One of the key factors that drew John to CEFs was their long history of paying distributions every month. Unlike other forms of passive income, such as rental properties or side businesses, John realized that investing in a diversified portfolio of CEFs required minimal ongoing effort.

By investing in CEFs, John achieved passive income without devoting significant time and labor to generate returns. Despite the inherent risks involved, he felt confident in managing these risks by diversifying his portfolio and investing in well-established CEFs with a strong track record of performance.

John had heard about the power of compounding, but he only fully understood it once he started investing in CEFs. He knew that by reinvesting his monthly dividends into his portfolio, he could take advantage of the power of compounding and maximize his returns over time.

One CEF that John had invested in was the PDT - John Hancock Premium Dividend Fund. Initially, he had invested $100,000, and the fund's annual distribution yield was 7.7% or $7,700 annually.

But John was in it for the long haul. He decided to reinvest his monthly dividends into the fund to buy more shares. He knew that the power of compounding would work in his favor over time.

After ten years of reinvesting his dividends into the fund, John's monthly distribution had increased significantly. He received $1,506 monthly in tips, nearly double his original monthly distribution of $771.

Money is a curious thing. It's only a tool we use to pursue happiness, yet somehow, many of us become slaves to it. We chase after it, work hard to earn it, and often need to catch up on what matters.

But what if we could turn the tables and become the master of money? Let's make it work for us instead of the other way around.

This is the beauty of dividend investment tools like closed-end funds. They allow us to harness the power of money and truly let it work for us. We no longer have to be accountable for the constant grind of earning and saving. Instead, we can invest in these tools, watch as our money grows, and earn a passive income.

It's like we've stumbled upon a secret, a hidden treasure that allows us to break free from the chains of financial worry and insecurity. We can invest our money and know that it's working for us, even when we're not actively working for it.

And it's not just about the money itself; it's about what that money can do for us. It can allow us to pursue our passions, spend time with our loved ones, travel the world, and experience all life offers.

The power of compounding means that our passive income streams can grow and grow over time, allowing us to achieve financial freedom and control over our time. It's a beautiful thing—the ability to let money work for us so we can focus on what truly matters in life.

So let us not be slaves to money any longer. Let us take charge and become the master of our finances.

With tools like closed-end funds and dividend investing, we can genuinely let money work for us and pursue the happiness and freedom we all deserve.

Chapter 12: Beyond Appearances: The True Nature of Wealth

Marcus Smith was a stoic man who valued wisdom and virtue over material possessions. Alexander Davis was a wealthy man born into a family of entrepreneurs. He spent his fortune on flashy cars, jewelry, and watches to impress others. Despite their differences, they remained acquaintances for years.

One day, they met at a social event and began chatting.

Alexander: "Marcus, have you seen my new car? It's a limited-edition Ferrari. I just had to have it!"

Marcus: "That's impressive, Alexander, but what good is a car if it doesn't get you anywhere meaningful?"

Alexander: "What do you mean? It's a Ferrari! It gets me everywhere I need to go in style."

Sophia Lee, a fashion blogger who admired Alexander's wealth and status, overheard their conversation and interjected.

Sophia: "I completely agree, Alexander. You should flaunt your possessions more often. It's what sets you apart from everyone else."

Marcus: "But what's the point of setting yourself apart if it doesn't bring you any real respect or admiration? Those things are earned through humility, kindness, and empathy, not through material possessions."

David Johnson, a humble mechanic who overheard the conversation, chimed in.

David: "I completely agree with Marcus. I may not have a lot of money, but I have the respect and admiration of my friends and family because I treat everyone with kindness and respect."

A successful businesswoman who shared Marcus's values, Olivia Williams, joined the conversation.

Olivia: "I completely agree. Money and status are temporary, but being a good person is what truly sets you apart and earns you respect."

Emily Martinez, a socialite who enjoyed the company of wealthy and influential people, joined the conversation and scoffed.

Emily: "You guys are missing the point. Money and status are what matter in this world. You have to show off your wealth if you want to be respected and admired."

As the night went on, Marcus's message stuck with everyone in the room. Alexander realized that his spending habits only brought him shallow admiration and that genuine respect and admiration come from humility and kindness. Sophia realized that her affection for Alexander's wealth was misguided and that proper care comes from being good. And Emily, well, she continued to chase after status and wealth, never realizing the true value of virtue and wisdom.

In the end, Marcus's stoic philosophy touched the lives of those around him, reminding them that pursuing material possessions and status may bring less respect and admiration than they imagined. Humility, kindness, and empathy bring people together and earn their respect.

The irony is that while we often associate wealth with expensive cars, luxurious homes, and designer clothes, true wealth lies in the things that can't be bought with money.

Wealth is the love and support of our family and friends, the satisfaction we get from doing meaningful work, and the joy we feel when we make a difference in the lives of others. Wealth is the ability to appreciate the simple things in life, like a beautiful sunset or a warm embrace from a loved one.

Money can buy material possessions but can't buy happiness, love, or fulfillment. The accurate measure of wealth is not in what we have but in who we are and how we choose to live.

The perspective on wealth is multifaceted, recognizing that material possessions can bring positive and negative outcomes. From a practical standpoint, it is acknowledged that wealth is impermanent and ultimately unsatisfying. Accumulating material possessions may get temporary pleasure but cannot bring lasting happiness or contentment. Detachment from material possessions is encouraged to avoid suffering and cultivate inner peace.

The potential of wealth to inspire positive qualities in people, such as generosity, kindness, and compassion, is also recognized. Giving is seen as a means to practice generosity, help others, and cultivate positive emotions. The act of giving is beneficial not only for the recipient but also for the giver. Generosity boosts positive emotions, such as joy, gratitude, and contentment, contributing to mental and emotional well-being.

At the same time, excessive attachment to wealth or material possessions is cautioned against. Such passion can lead to negative emotions such as greed, envy, and jealousy, which can cause mental and emotional distress. It can also hinder spiritual growth and enlightenment, as it can distract from the true nature of reality.

Pursuing wealth can lead to a false sense of security and happiness, which can be shattered by unexpected events such as illness, death, or loss. Retaining from material possessions can help develop a sense of stability and acceptance in the face of change and uncertainty. By recognizing the impermanence of material possessions, greater peace and happiness can be found in life.

Nicolas Cage was once one of Hollywood's highest-paid actors, earning millions for each film he starred in. However, his extravagant spending habits and risky investments eventually caught up with him, leading to financial troubles and near bankruptcy.

Cage's financial woes began in the early 2000s when he went on a spending spree, buying lavish homes, cars, and collectibles. He reportedly owned multiple castles, a private island, a fleet of exotic cars, and a collection of rare comic books. Cage even outbid Leonardo DiCaprio for a dinosaur skull at an auction, paying over $276,000 for the unique artifact.

Despite his massive earnings, Cage's extravagant lifestyle and bad investments eventually led to financial trouble. He faced several lawsuits and unpaid taxes, and his real estate empire began to crumble. He reportedly owed millions of dollars in delinquent taxes and loans and was forced to sell many of his assets to pay off his debts.

In 2009, Cage sued his former business manager for fraud and mismanagement, claiming that he had squandered Cage's fortune on bad investments and excessive fees. Cage ultimately settled the lawsuit for an undisclosed amount, but his financial troubles continued.

In 2010, Cage was forced to sell several properties, including his Bel Air mansion and a Bavarian castle. He also had to auction off many prized possessions, including his comic book collection and shrunken heads.

Today, Cage has reportedly restructured his finances and is working to rebuild his wealth. However, his experiences are a cautionary tale about the dangers of excessive spending and bad investments, even for those earning millions in Hollywood.

Entrepreneurship and making money are good. They can be powerful tools for creating positive change in society. However, it is essential to consider how we perceive, manage, and use money.

Money has a significant impact on our lives and the world around us. It can build businesses, fund research, and support charitable causes. On the other hand, it can fuel greed and selfishness, leading to negative consequences for individuals and society.

Therefore, it is crucial to approach money with a mindset of responsibility and purpose. This means understanding the value of money beyond its purchasing power and being mindful of how our financial decisions impact others.

How we perceive, manage, and use money reflects our values and priorities. By taking a thoughtful approach to our finances, we can positively impact the world and create a more just and equitable society.

A psychological experiment conducted by Leaf Van Boven and Thomas Gilovich in 2003 provides evidence that using money to pursue excessive material possessions can lead to short-lived happiness. In this study, participants were asked to rate their level of satisfaction before and after purchasing either a material item, such as clothing or electronics, or an experiential item, such as concert tickets or a weekend getaway.

The results showed that while participants initially reported higher happiness levels after purchasing a material item, the pleasure quickly faded and returned to pre-purchase levels within weeks. On the other hand, those who bought an experiential item reported sustained levels of happiness long after the experience had ended.

The researchers suggest that this is because material possessions are subject to adaptation effects, which means that we quickly become accustomed to their presence. The pleasure we derive from them wears off. In contrast, experiences are more likely to remain pleasurable memories that we can reflect upon and savor for longer.

Therefore, this study suggests that investing in experiences may be a more fulfilling and satisfying use of our financial resources than pursuing excessive material possessions. It implies that using money to buy material possessions may not lead to sustained happiness, whereas investing in experiences can lead to long-lasting positive feelings.

Warren Buffett was an investor with a net worth of over $100 billion who still lived in the same modest house he had purchased for $31,500 in 1958. He also drove a simple car and enjoyed eating at fast-food restaurants. Mark Zuckerberg was a tech entrepreneur with a net worth of over $100 billion who famously wore the same gray t-shirt and jeans to work every day and drove a basic Volkswagen hatchback. Kristen Bell was an actress known for her roles in popular TV shows and movies, but she still took a 2004 Lexus SUV and shopped at discount stores like Costco and Marshalls. Ingvar Kamprad was the founder of IKEA with a net worth of over $50 billion who flew economy class, drove an old Volvo, and lived in a modest home.

These celebrities lived frugally despite their wealth, demonstrating that they pursued wealth with a higher meaning and purpose. They understood that material possessions did not necessarily equate to happiness or fulfillment. By living frugally, they could focus on their goals and make meaningful contributions to society rather than being distracted by materialistic pursuits.

Warren Buffett had always believed in living modestly, even before becoming one of the world's wealthiest people. He once said, "I don't have a boat, I don't have a plane, I have everything I need." For him, money was a tool to invest in companies and create shareholder value. He also believed in giving back to society, pledging to donate most of his wealth to philanthropic causes through the Giving Pledge.

Mark Zuckerberg had a similar philosophy, focusing on the mission of Facebook to connect people around the world rather than on his wealth. He once said, "I'm here to build something for the long term. Anything else is a distraction." He and his wife, Priscilla Chan, established the Chan Zuckerberg Initiative to invest in education, science, and other causes.

Kristen Bell grew up in a family that struggled financially, so she learned to be frugal early. She prioritized her family and charitable giving over material possessions, saying, "I'm more interested in making sure my daughters have the education they need than I am in having a fancy car." She supported causes like education, animal rights, and mental health.

Ingvar Kamprad had always believed in the power of frugality and simplicity. He had started IKEA to provide affordable furniture to the masses, using leftover wood to create the iconic flat-pack furniture the company is known for. He believed in living a modest lifestyle, saying, "I have never been interested in being flashy. I prefer to stay in the background."

These four celebrities demonstrated that pursuing wealth with a higher meaning and purpose is possible, focusing on goals beyond material possessions. By living frugally, they were able to stay true to their values and make a positive impact on the world.

In today's world, judging others based on their outward appearance and making assumptions about their success or financial status is easy. We may see someone driving a fancy car or wearing expensive clothes and assume they are wealthy while overlooking the possibility of living beyond their means and struggling with debt. Conversely, we may encounter someone who appears modest and unassuming and assumes they are only successful by realizing they may have accumulated wealth through intelligent investments or frugal living.

This tendency to judge others quickly based on appearances can harm us and others. It can lead us to set unrealistic goals based on materialistic aspirations rather than pursuing what truly matters to us. It can also lead us to overlook the achievements and accomplishments of those who do not fit our preconceived notions of success.

Therefore, it is crucial to be mindful of our biases and assumptions when evaluating others' success and setting goals. We should strive to focus on our values and priorities rather than comparing ourselves to others or trying to keep up with the Joneses. We should also seek to learn from those who may not fit our stereotype of success, recognizing that there are many paths to achieving financial security and fulfillment.

Chapter 13: You See What You Want to See

A saying goes, "You see what you want to see." It's a statement that speaks volumes about how our minds work, especially regarding the things we desire. When we want something badly enough, we tend to believe stories that overestimate the odds of it coming true. It's a human tendency that has been observed time and time again, and it's a fascinating one at that.

There's no denying the power of desire. It can drive us to accomplish great things, chase after our dreams, and never give up on what we want. But there's a flip side to this too. Sometimes, when we want something too much, we can become blinded by our desires and start to believe things that aren't necessarily true.

It's like a self-fulfilling prophecy. The more we want something to be accurate, the more likely we are to believe in stories that support that desire. It's a trap that many of us fall into, and it can be dangerous. We can start to ignore evidence to the contrary and become so fixated on our desires that we lose sight of reality.

This is why we must be aware of our biases and challenge our beliefs. We need to be open to the possibility that what we want might not be best for us, and we need to be willing to accept the truth, even if it's not what we want to hear.

It's a delicate balance, to be sure. We don't want to give up on our dreams, but we also don't want to be deluded by them. We must find a way to hold onto our desires without letting them control us. It's a challenge, but it's worth taking on.

In the early 2000s, a man named John Deuss, a Dutch oil trader invested heavily in a company called Bayoil USA. The company claimed access to vast oil reserves in Nigeria and promised to deliver high returns on investment.

Deuss was already wealthy, but he wanted to become even richer. He believed the stories of Bayoil's success and invested millions of dollars in the company.

Deuss refused to believe that Bayoil was anything but a successful and profitable business, even though other investors had warned him and financial regulators had their doubts. He continued to pour money into the company, convinced that his investments would pay off.

In 2007, Bayoil was exposed as a massive fraud. The company had been falsifying documents and lying about its oil reserves for years. John Deuss lost everything he had invested in the company and was charged with fraud.

John Deuss's story is a tragic reminder of how our desires can blind us to the truth and how stories can manipulate people's beliefs. It's a cautionary tale that shows how important it is to think critically and question our biases and assumptions, especially regarding our money and investments.

In 1849 the news had just arrived: gold had been discovered in California. It was a dream come true for many, a promise of unimaginable wealth and prosperity. People from all over the world flocked to California, driven by the stories of gold.

As they arrived, they found land in chaos. The once-quiet hills were now teeming with life, with thousands of people searching for gold. The air was thick with the sound of pickaxes and the rush of the rivers where they panned for gold.

The stories of gold became more exaggerated with each passing day. People started to believe that gold could be found anywhere and was waiting to be picked up off the ground. Some even thought there was a secret location where gold could be found in vast quantities.

The competition was fierce, and people were willing to do anything to strike it rich. They risked their lives in the dangerous mines and rivers, hoping to find gold. Some were lucky and struck it rich, but most were not so fortunate.

Despite the hardships and disappointments, people continued to believe in the stories of gold. They clung to the hope of striking it rich and refused to give up. The stories of the California Gold Rush became a legend, a symbol of hope, and a reminder of the human desire for wealth.

But as the years went by, the gold rush faded. The stories lost their magic, and people began to see the reality of the situation. Many had spent their life savings on the journey to California, only to find that the truth was much harsher than the stories had led them to believe.

The California Gold Rush remains a significant event in American history, a testament to the power of human desire and the enduring allure of wealth.

Investing can be risky and uncertain, yet many people still tune in to TV investment commentary for insights and tips. The stakes are high, and the possibility of getting rich quickly with a few stock picks is alluring. It's like standing on the edge of a cliff, looking out at a vast, unexplored landscape, and imagining all the possibilities.

The problem is that the odds of success are often low, and the risk of failure is high. But the desire for wealth and success is so strong that people are willing to take that risk, hoping for a miracle.

The allure of investing is like a siren's call, tempting and irresistible. It's like a game of chance, where the potential rewards are so great that they overshadow the risks. The possibility of striking it rich with a single investment is a dream many people share, and they will do whatever it takes to make it a reality.

The problem is that this dream can become an obsession, blinding people to the reality of the situation. They become invested in their financial and mental beliefs and refuse to consider the possibility of failure. They cling to their strategies and opinions, hoping that they will be proven right in the end.

But the truth is that investing is not always a good thing. There are always risks, and success is never guaranteed. It's like sailing on a stormy sea, with no clear path and no certainty of reaching your destination. Yet people still drift on, hoping to reach the other side and find the treasure they seek.

The stock market is like a vast ocean, teeming with life and possibilities. It's a world of high-stakes gambling, where fortunes are won and lost on a dice roll. And yet, people continue to flock to the market, hoping to strike it rich with their investments.

The problem is that the odds are never in their favor. The data shows that most individual investors underperform the market over the long term. Despite this, people still believe they can beat the odds and succeed.

It's like a fisherman casting his net into the sea, hoping to catch a prize fish. He knows that the odds are against him, but the allure of the catch is too strong to resist. He keeps casting, hoping the following catch will be the big one.

But the reality is that the fisherman is likely to catch something of value. The market is too unpredictable and volatile to rely on as a sure source of income. Yet people continue to invest, hoping for that big catch that will change their lives forever.

It's like a gambler at a casino, hoping to hit the jackpot with a single spin of the wheel. He knows the odds are against him, but the possibility of a huge payout is too strong to ignore. He keeps spinning, hoping the next spin will be the lucky one.

One of the most infamous scammers in history is Charles Ponzi, whose scheme was so effective that his name now knows it. In the early 1900s, Ponzi convinced thousands of people to invest in his scheme, promising enormous returns from buying and selling international postage stamps.

Even though Ponzi's scheme was mathematically impossible and he had no legitimate means of generating returns, people continued to invest in it. They were seduced by the allure of the promised returns, which were much higher than anything they could get elsewhere.

Ponzi was a master of storytelling, and he told his investors precisely what they wanted to hear. He painted a picture of a world where wealth was easy to come by, and they could all be millionaires if they had just invested with him. And people believed him, even when there were signs of something wrong.

It's like a magician performing a trick, distracting his audience with one hand while the other does the real work. Ponzi was a master of distraction, using his storytelling abilities to distract his investors from the reality of the situation.

But in the end, the truth always comes out. Ponzi's scheme eventually collapsed, and he was exposed as a fraud. Many of his investors lost everything they had invested, and their dreams of wealth and success were shattered.

The world is like a giant puzzle, with millions of pieces that don't always fit perfectly. It's a complex and confusing place, full of contradictions and inconsistencies. And yet, we humans have an innate desire to make sense of it all, to find patterns and connections where there may be none.

The problem is that our desire to make sense of the world can often lead us astray. We look back at history and think that we understand it and that we can explain it, but the truth is that hindsight is always 20/20. We see things that were once hidden and believe we could have predicted them all along.

It's like a detective solving a crime, piecing together clues and evidence to create a coherent narrative. The detective thinks that he understands what happened, but the truth is that there may be other explanations that he still needs to consider. He may be blinded by his own biases and assumptions, seeing what he wants to see rather than what is there.

Or it's like a composer creating a symphony, weaving together different melodies and harmonies to create a beautiful whole. The composer thinks that he understands the music he has created, but the truth is that there may be other interpretations that he still needs to consider. He may be deaf to the nuances and complexities of the piece, hearing only what he wants to hear.

A psychologist named Daniel Kahneman had a theory about human decision-making. He called it "prospect theory," It was all about how people are motivated by the potential for gain rather than the potential for loss.

Kahneman's theory helped explain why people often make irrational choices and are susceptible to biases and illusions. It showed that people are more likely to take risks when there is a chance of a big payoff, even if the odds are low. On the other hand, they are more risk-averse when faced with the possibility of a loss.

Kahneman's theory also explains why people are susceptible to biases and illusions. They rely on mental shortcuts or heuristics when making decisions, which can lead to errors in judgment. They may also be influenced by emotions and other external factors, which can cloud their judgment and lead them to make poor choices.

The allure of quick riches is a powerful force that has led many investors down a dangerous path. When certain high-risk stocks, such as small tech stocks, start to climb rapidly, people's hopes soar, and they become convinced that they can get rich quickly. They begin to intentionally seek out biased news that supports their beliefs, ignoring any negative information that might spoil their hopes.

One such example is the story of Theranos, a healthcare technology company that promised to revolutionize the blood testing industry. The company's founder, Elizabeth Holmes, became a media darling and was touted as the next Steve Jobs. Investors poured millions of dollars into the company, with some valuing it at over $9 billion.

However, it was later revealed that Theranos still needed to develop a working product and had misled investors and the public about its capabilities. The company's value plummeted, and Holmes was charged with multiple counts of fraud.

Another example is the rise and fall of the cryptocurrency market. Many investors were lured in by the promise of huge returns from investing in Bitcoin and other digital currencies. The market soared in value, with some cryptocurrencies reaching astronomical prices. However, the market was highly volatile, and many investors lost significant amounts of money when the market crashed. Whenever great investors like Warren Buffet and Charlie Munger expressed their views that cryptocurrency had no intrinsic value, many would angrily retort that these two men were already old and did not understand new things; this time was different. Well, the truth is: this time is the same.

The dot-com bubble of the early 2000s is the most famous example of the dangers of chasing overvalued high-risk stocks. Many tech companies became overvalued, and investors poured billions of dollars into them, hoping to cash in on their potential. However, when the bubble burst in 2000, many companies went bankrupt, and investors lost billions of dollars.

More recently, the rise and fall of EV stocks have been a cautionary tale of the risks involved in investing in high-risk stocks. In 2020, Tesla's stock price soared by over 700%, while other EV companies like NIO and Workhorse saw their prices rise by over 1,000%. However, these stocks were incredibly volatile, and in early 2021, many saw significant value declines. For example, NIO's stock price fell by over 30% in just one day, wiping out billions of dollars in market value.

Perhaps, the best way to ensure safety and consistent returns is to follow Warren Buffett's advice:

- Invest in a low-cost S&P 500 index fund.
- Be patient.
- Let time and compounding work for you.

It is helpful to remind all of us of some most famous quotes from Warren Buffet to end this chapter:

1. "Rule No. 1: Never lose money. Rule No. 2: Never forget Rule No. 1."
2. "Be fearful when others are greedy, and greedy when others are fearful."
3. "It's far better to buy a wonderful company at a fair price than a fair company at a wonderful price."
4. "Our favorite holding period is forever."
5. "Price is what you pay. Value is what you get."

6. “Risk comes from not knowing what you're doing.”
7. “The stock market is a device for transferring money from the impatient to the patient.”
8. “The best investment you can make is in yourself.”
9. “I will tell you how to become rich. Close the doors.”
10. “The difference between successful people and really successful people is that really successful people say no to almost everything.”

Chapter 14: Asymmetrical Risk/Reward: How to Win Big by Being Wrong More Often

George Washington was pivotal in the American Revolution, leading the Continental Army against the mighty British Army. However, his path to victory could have been smoother, and he faced numerous setbacks and defeats.

At the outbreak of the war, Washington was a respected military leader, having served in the French and Indian War and as a delegate to the Continental Congress. He was appointed commander-in-chief of the Continental Army in 1775, but he soon faced a formidable opponent in the British Army.

Washington's first major battle was at Bunker Hill, where the Continental Army suffered heavy losses. Despite this defeat, Washington remained committed to his cause and continued to fight.

In the summer of 1776, Washington faced his greatest challenge as the British launched a major offensive in New York. The Battle of Long Island was a significant defeat for the Continental Army, resulting in the loss of New York City and a retreat to Pennsylvania.

The following year, Washington faced another defeat at the Battle of Brandywine, which saw the

British capture Philadelphia. Washington's army was forced to retreat to Valley Forge, where they met harsh winter conditions and a shortage of supplies.

Despite these setbacks, Washington remained steadfast in his determination to win the war. He adopted a strategy of attrition, wearing down the British Army through small-scale skirmishes and surprise attacks.

Finally, in 1781, Washington saw his chance to strike a decisive blow against the British at the Battle of Yorktown. With the help of his French allies, Washington was able to trap the British Army, leading to their eventual surrender.

The Battle of Yorktown marked the war's turning point, and it would not have been possible without Washington's leadership and strategic genius. He emerged from the war as a hero and was elected the first President of the United States.

Washington's military campaign had flaws, and he faced numerous challenges. However, his leadership and unwavering commitment to his cause were instrumental in securing America's independence.

In business and investing, failure is common, and many entrepreneurs and investors face multiple setbacks before finally achieving their goals. Like how Washington faced numerous defeats before winning the Battle of Yorktown, many investors and entrepreneurs failed many times before achieving success.

The venture capital industry operates on the principle of high risk and high reward. Venture capitalists invest in early-stage companies with high growth potential but are also highly risky. They know that most startups fail but are willing to take the risk because the few startups that succeed can bring enormous returns.

In the 1980s, Apple struggled to compete with IBM, and the company's products needed to gain traction in the market. Apple's co-founder, Steve Jobs, left the company in 1985, and the company's future looked uncertain.

In the years that followed, Apple struggled to find its footing. The company launched a series of unsuccessful products, including the Apple III, the Apple Lisa, and the Macintosh Portable. These products were commercial failures, and Apple's financial performance suffered.

However, in 1997, Apple made a bold move that would change the company's fortunes forever. The company brought back Steve Jobs as CEO, and he quickly set to work revitalizing the company's product lineup.

Under Jobs' leadership, Apple launched a series of groundbreaking products that transformed the technology industry. The iPod, launched in 2001, revolutionized how people listened to music. The iPhone, launched in 2007, redefined the smartphone industry. The iPad, established in 2010, created a new category of computing devices.

The success of these products turned Apple into one of the most valuable companies in the world, with a market capitalization that now exceeds $2 trillion.

In the early years of Amazon, the company struggled to profit. The company launched a series of unsuccessful products and services, including Amazon Auctions and Amazon's WebPay, failing to gain market traction.

Despite these setbacks, Amazon's founder and CEO, Jeff Bezos, remained committed to creating a company that would transform how people shop online. He believed that Amazon had the potential to become a global force in e-commerce, and he was determined to make it happen.

To achieve his vision, Bezos continued to innovate and take risks. He launched Amazon Prime, a subscription service offering customers free shipping and other perks, and introduced the Kindle. This revolutionary e-reader transformed the way people read books.

However, Amazon's biggest success came with the launch of Amazon Web Services (AWS), a cloud computing platform that allows businesses to store and access data and applications on remote servers. AWS was a game changer for the technology industry, and it quickly became one of the most profitable divisions of Amazon.

While companies like Apple and Amazon have been able to persevere through failure and achieve great success, the reality is that only some companies make it to the level of success that these companies have achieved. Many companies, including once-successful companies that were part of the S&P 500, have failed and died out prematurely.

For example, some companies that were once part of the S&P 500 and no longer exist include Blockbuster Video, Kodak, Polaroid, and Circuit City. These were all once successful companies that failed to adapt to changing market conditions and consumer preferences, ultimately leading to their demise.

Moreover, the failure rate among new businesses is high as well. According to the Small Business Administration, only about half of new businesses survive beyond their first five years, and only one-third survive beyond their tenth year.

According to a study by Innosight, a global strategic innovation consulting firm, the average lifespan of a company listed on the S&P 500 decreased from 61 years in 1958 to 18 years in 2012. This means that companies are failing more frequently and that the average lifespan of a company has been decreasing over time.

The Innosight study on the average lifespan of S&P 500 companies analyzed historical data from 1958 to 2016. The study found that the rate at which companies are being replaced on the index has been accelerating. The average lifespan of a company listed on the S&P 500 has decreased.

Specifically, the study found that in 1965, the average lifespan of a company on the S&P 500 was 33 years. By 1990, this had decreased to 20 years, and by 2016, the average lifespan of a company on the S&P 500 was just 24 years.

The study also found that the number of companies being replaced on the index has increased. Between 1958 and 1965, an average of 20 companies were replaced on the index yearly. By the early 2000s, this had risen to an average of 50 companies per year; by 2016, the replacement rate had reached an all-time high of 75 companies per year.

The study identified several factors contributing to the decreasing lifespan of S&P 500 companies, including rapid advances in technology, globalization, and changing consumer preferences. Companies that cannot adapt to these changes risk being replaced on the index by more agile and innovative competitors.

According to another source, data from Siblis Research, a financial data and analytics firm, the total number of companies that have been part of the S&P 500 index since 1957 is approximately 1,740. Of these companies, about 60% have been replaced by other companies or have gone bankrupt or been acquired by other companies.

Despite the high failure rate of S&P 500 companies, Warren Buffett, one of the most successful investors in history, has consistently recommended that ordinary people invest a significant portion of their assets in S&P 500 index funds.

Buffett has long been a proponent of index funds, mutual funds, or ETFs that track the performance of a specific stock market index, such as the S&P 500. He has argued that index funds provide investors with a simple and low-cost way to invest in the stock market and that they have historically outperformed most actively managed funds.

Moreover, Buffett has consistently recommended the S&P 500 index as a good option for long-term investors. He has argued that the S&P 500 provides investors with exposure to a diversified portfolio of large-cap U.S. stocks and has historically delivered solid returns over the long term.

Buffett has stated that after he dies, he has instructed the trustees of his estate to invest 90% of his assets in S&P 500 index funds. This is a testament to his belief in the long-term potential of the S&P 500 and his confidence in the ability of index funds to deliver solid returns over the long term.

Investing in the S&P 500 index has historically been profitable for long-term investors. According to data from Yahoo Finance, the average annual return of the S&P 500 index since 1945 has been approximately 10%, including dividends.

If an investor had invested $10,000 in the S&P 500 index in 1945 and reinvested all dividends, their investment would have grown to approximately $51 million by the end of 2020. This extraordinary return on investment demonstrates the long-term growth potential of investing in the stock market.

The experience of the S&P 500 index demonstrates that even if an investor makes mistakes and is wrong a significant percentage of the time, they can still achieve substantial returns on their investment over the long term.

By investing in a diversified portfolio of stocks, such as the S&P 500 index, investors can minimize their exposure to individual company risk and benefit from the long-term growth potential of the stock market.

While individual companies may experience setbacks and failures, the stock market has historically delivered solid returns over the long term. By remaining patient and disciplined and investing for the long term, investors can increase their chances of achieving significant returns on their investment, even if they make mistakes.

Peter Lynch, the former manager of the Fidelity Magellan Fund, was renowned for his successful track record as an investor. Over his tenure from 1977 to 1990, he generated annualized returns of over 29% for the fund, a feat that had never been accomplished before

But many people may not know that only a handful of Lynch's investments were responsible for the bulk of the fund's overall return. He estimated that only about 25% of the fund's investments were genuinely accountable for its success.

Lynch acknowledged this fact in a speech at the Harvard Business School in 1995. He explained that while many investors focus on diversifying their portfolio and spreading their investments across a wide range of companies, the reality is that only a few key investments can truly make a difference in one's overall returns.

"If you had taken the top 25 holdings out of Magellan, the results would have been terrible,"

Lynch said. "You'd have lost money, in fact, if you took the top 50 out."

This revelation may surprise some investors, who may assume that a successful portfolio requires many successful investments. But for Lynch, the key was identifying high-quality companies with strong growth potential and focusing on those investments, even if they represented only a tiny percentage of the overall portfolio.

Moreover, Lynch emphasized the importance of maintaining a long-term investment horizon and avoiding the temptation to chase short-term market trends or make impulsive investment decisions.

"If you can't hold onto a stock for five years, don't even think about owning it for five minutes," Lynch said.

Investing is a journey through a vast, ever-changing landscape of unpredictable twists and turns. But like any journey, well-trodden paths often lead to success.

One such path is investing in a broad-based index fund like the S&P 500. While the individual companies within the index may rise and fall over time, the overall market trend is growth and prosperity.

Investors who stay the course and hold on through market turbulence can reap the rewards of this long-term trend. Even if some individual companies within the index fail, the collective strength of the remaining companies can still deliver significant returns.

It's like hiking through a rugged wilderness. While the path may be rocky and strenuous, following a well-worn trail can lead to breathtaking vistas and stunning natural beauty. Similarly, investing in an index fund can be a reliable guide through the ups and downs of the market, leading investors to a landscape of long-term growth and prosperity.

So while the journey of investing may be uncertain and unpredictable, those who stay the course and follow the well-trodden paths of the market can achieve great success over the long term.

Chapter 15: Being Flexible

A young woman named Emily hailed from a humble background and faced many obstacles in life. Despite the challenges, she was determined to make something of herself and worked tirelessly to fulfill her dreams. Her unwavering ambition was to become a renowned chef in a world-class restaurant. The odds were against her, but she persevered.

As the years went by, Emily gradually climbed the ladder of success, working her way through every station in the kitchen. Eventually, she reached the pinnacle of her profession, and her dream became a reality. Her dedication and hard work had finally paid off.

One day, I happened to bump into Emily after a long time. Excited to catch up, I asked, "Hey, Emily, it's been ages! How's life as a top chef?"

Her response took me aback. "You know what?" she sighed. "It's not what I imagined it to be."

Confused, I asked her to elaborate. Emily described how the long hours, the pressure to maintain excellence, and the constant competition had worn her down. She had achieved her dream, but the reality of her success was far from what she had envisioned.

This story illustrates our everyday struggle when trying to predict our future selves. We often fixate on our goals without considering the challenges and sacrifices accompanying our pursuits. This lack of foresight can lead to disillusionment and a disconnect between our dreams and the reality of achieving them. This inability to accurately anticipate the future also extends to our financial planning, making it crucial to approach our goals with a comprehensive understanding of the potential obstacles and realities.

Little Timmy was enamored with becoming a firefighter as a child. The thrill of riding in a big red truck, sirens blaring, was irresistible. As he grew older, however, his aspirations evolved. He began to dream of becoming an engineer, envisioning a prestigious and high-paying career. And so, he embarked on the challenging path towards his new goal, investing time and money into his education.

Upon achieving his dream, Timmy found that an engineer's long hours and high-stress environment took a toll on his personal life. Seeking a better work-life balance, he transitioned to a less demanding job with more flexible hours. As his family grew, he discovered the high costs of childcare, ultimately deciding to become a stay-at-home parent. This new role gave him the time and connection he craved with his family.

Years later, as Timmy approached retirement, he realized his career changes had left him financially unprepared for this next phase of life. Like many others, his journey was marked by unexpected twists and turns. Many college graduates don't work in fields related to their degrees, and many stay-at-home parents possess higher education qualifications. While these individuals may not regret their choices, their experiences highlight that our goals and desires shift as we navigate life.

Long-term financial planning is crucial, but we must acknowledge that the future is uncertain and subject to our ever-changing wants and needs. The challenge lies in making lasting decisions when we cannot predict how our preferences and circumstances will evolve. Recognizing this inherent fluidity is essential in creating flexible, adaptable financial plans that weather the shifting landscape of our lives.

The "Continual Evolution Conundrum" refers to the common human tendency to recognize how much we have changed throughout our lives while underestimating the extent to which our personalities, desires, and goals will continue to transform in the future. This psychological phenomenon often leads us to make decisions that significantly impact our future selves without fully considering how our preferences might evolve.

For example, imagine someone in their early twenties investing considerable time and money into building a collection of rare sports memorabilia.

However, as they age, they may find that their interests have shifted, and the once-cherished group no longer holds the same value. Similarly, people often select their careers or life partners in their youth, only to later discover that their priorities have changed as they mature. We are under the illusion that we have reached our final form, despite the evidence that we will continue to evolve throughout our lives.

This inability to fully grasp our future transformation has significant implications for long-term financial planning. As legendary investor Warren Buffett advises, the key to successful investing is to be patient and let the power of compounding work its magic. However, maintaining a consistent financial plan can be challenging when our life goals and circumstances are constantly in flux.

One way to approach our financial lives is to view them as a series of distinct stages, each with unique priorities and challenges. By acknowledging that our desires and goals will naturally evolve, we can create more adaptable and resilient financial plans that account for the ever-changing nature of our lives. This approach allows us to be better prepared for the unexpected twists and turns that life inevitably brings, helping us achieve a more secure financial future.

Some young individuals embrace a minimalist lifestyle with limited income, finding genuine contentment in simplicity. On the other hand, some work tirelessly to afford a life of extravagance and find equal happiness in their choices. Both paths come with their challenges—the former may struggle to support a family or secure a comfortable retirement, while the latter may one day look back and lament the time spent confined to an office during their prime years.

By presenting this contrasting scenario, we can see that different people have different definitions of happiness and success. Each individual's choices and goals are shaped by their unique values and circumstances. It's important to recognize that there is more than a one-size-fits-all solution to finding fulfillment and financial security. Instead, we should strive to make informed decisions that align with our values and aspirations while being aware of the potential risks and trade-offs involved in our chosen paths.

It's essential to find a middle ground in financial planning. Believing that a meager income will suffice or doggedly pursuing a high income can lead to disillusionment in the future. The danger of the "Continual Evolution Conundrum" lies in the fact that individuals tend to adapt to their circumstances, causing the allure of extreme financial plans to diminish over time. As a result, the disadvantages of these powerful approaches—insufficient funds for retirement or a life consumed by the chase for wealth—can become lasting sources of regret.

Regret is particularly poignant when one abandons a previous plan, feeling compelled to double their efforts in the opposite direction to compensate for lost time. The power of compounding is most effective when allowed to thrive over years or even decades, a principle that applies not only to saving but also to careers and relationships. Perseverance is vital.

Considering our natural propensity to evolve, maintaining balance at each stage of life becomes a powerful strategy for averting future regrets and fostering perseverance. Striving to balance average savings, leisure time, manageable commutes, and quality family time throughout one's working life increases the likelihood of adhering to a long-term plan and minimizing regret, as opposed to adopting a revolutionary approach that may not be sustainable in the long run.

It's essential to come to terms with the fact that our preferences and decisions may evolve. Some of the most disenchanted individuals persist with a career solely because it was their choice when selecting their college major as a teenager. By recognizing the Continual Evolution Conundrum, we understand that it's unlikely for a career chosen at a young age to remain fulfilling as we approach retirement. The answer lies in acknowledging the reality of change and adapting as quickly as possible.

A prominent financial writer, who collaborated with a distinguished psychologist on a groundbreaking book, shared an intriguing story about his co-author's unique characteristic that greatly benefited their teamwork.

They would invest countless hours working on a chapter, only for the co-author to substantially revamp it, infusing it with innovative ideas and previously undiscovered research. When asked about his ability to start anew, the co-author offered a thought-provoking response: "I have no attachment to the past efforts."

Being overly attached to past efforts—decisions rooted in previous endeavors that cannot be reclaimed—is dangerous in a world where people constantly evolve. They chain our future selves to our past selves, essentially different individuals. It is akin to allowing a stranger to dictate important life choices for us. Accepting that financial goals set by your earlier self should be let go without guilt, rather than being artificially maintained, can be an effective strategy to minimize future regret. The faster this is achieved, the sooner one can harness the power of compounding.

Chapter 16: The Harms of Comparison

In biology, our propensity to compare ourselves to others can be traced back to our evolutionary roots. As social animals, humans have relied on group dynamics for survival. Previously, being part of a group meant increased chances of finding food, securing shelter, and fending off predators. As a result, our ancestors developed a keen awareness of their position within the group hierarchy. This instinct to compare ourselves to others has persisted through generations, leading us to measure our success and self-worth against those around us.

From a psychological perspective, social comparison can be both a motivating and demoralizing force. On the one hand, comparing ourselves to others can inspire us to work harder and achieve more. Witnessing the accomplishments of our peers can motivate us to strive for similar successes, pushing us to reach our full potential. However, this same comparison can also be the source of our discontent. When we perceive others as having achieved more than us, we may experience feelings of inadequacy or envy. These emotions can be detrimental to our mental health and overall happiness, as they foster a sense of dissatisfaction with our own lives.

Socially, our modern world has amplified the effects of comparison through the widespread use of social media. Platforms like Facebook, Instagram, and Twitter offer a constant stream of curated images and stories that depict the idealized lives of others. As we scroll through these images, we may make subconscious comparisons, internalize feelings of inferiority, and grow increasingly dissatisfied with our lives. The constant exposure to others' perceived success can make it difficult for us to appreciate our accomplishments and focus on our personal growth.

To counteract the adverse effects of comparison, we can turn to the principles of mindfulness and gratitude. Mindfulness encourages us to be present in the moment, allowing us to appreciate the beauty of our current circumstances without constantly seeking more. By focusing on the present, we can recognize and celebrate the small, everyday victories that contribute to our overall happiness. Conversely, gratitude helps us cultivate a deeper appreciation for the good things in our lives. By actively practicing gratitude, we can shift our focus from what we lack to what we have, fostering a sense of contentment and fulfillment.

In many cultures, success and happiness are often defined by specific milestones, such as obtaining a prestigious job, earning a high salary, or having a picture-perfect family. These societal benchmarks can contribute to our tendency to compare ourselves to others, as they create a framework for measuring our achievements.

Cultural norms and expectations can vary widely between societies, yet they all share a common thread: the pressure to conform and achieve the prescribed markers of success. This pressure can exacerbate our innate tendency to compare ourselves to others, causing us to feel inadequate when we do not meet these societal standards. Moreover, pursuing these external markers of success can lead us to prioritize the wrong aspects of our lives, sacrificing our personal growth and well-being.

To break free from societal expectations and comparison constraints, we must challenge the cultural norms that dictate our definitions of success and happiness. By redefining what success means to us individually, we can focus on our values and priorities, paving the way for a more authentic and fulfilling life. Embracing our unique paths and celebrating our achievements, rather than comparing ourselves to others, can ultimately lead to greater contentment and a more profound sense of self-worth.

In celebrities, wealth and success can often become a point of comparison and competition. Consider a fictional story involving six famous individuals, each with impressive earnings.

Emma Stone, a talented actress, has enjoyed a prosperous career, earning an estimated $26 million in 2017. However, upon attending a prestigious Hollywood event, she found herself in the company of Dwayne "The Rock" Johnson, who boasted earnings of $87.5 million in 2020. As Emma compared her income to Dwayne's, she couldn't help but feel envy.

At the same gathering, Dwayne Johnson conversed with Kylie Jenner, the successful businesswoman and reality TV star, who revealed that she had earned a staggering $590 million in 2020. Although content with his accomplishments, Dwayne felt inadequate when comparing his earnings to Kylie's vast fortune.

As the evening progressed, Kylie Jenner spoke with Oprah Winfrey, the highly influential media mogul and philanthropist. Upon discovering that Oprah's net worth had reached an estimated $3.5 billion in 2021, Kylie couldn't help but feel a little overshadowed by her immense wealth.

During a moment of respite, Oprah Winfrey spoke with Jeff Bezos, the founder and former CEO of Amazon. To Oprah's surprise, Bezos revealed that his net worth had peaked at $177 billion in 2021. Despite her incredible success, Oprah was reminded that others had amassed even greater fortunes.

Finally, Bernard Arnault, the French billionaire and CEO of LVMH, joined the gathering. Arnault surpassed Bezos' wealth with a net worth of around $193 billion in 2021. Despite Bezos' numerous achievements, he couldn't help but feel a sense of rivalry with Arnault.

In this fictional scenario, each successful individual compares their wealth to one another, feeling jealousy and dissatisfaction. This story demonstrates that regardless of how much money one earns, someone will always have more incredible wealth. These celebrities may struggle to find true contentment and happiness through this constant comparison cycle. Instead, focusing on personal achievements and fostering gratitude for what they have could lead to a more fulfilling existence.

Once upon a time, in a world where East and West met, a group of renowned philosophers and spiritual teachers gathered to discuss the nature of human happiness. Among them were Schopenhauer, a Stoic philosopher, a Buddhist monk, and many other figures representing various traditions.

As they sat around a table, sipping tea and engaging in lively conversation, the subject of desire and comparison arose. Schopenhauer, a Western philosopher known for his pessimistic views, started by sharing his thoughts. He believed that desire was the root of all suffering and that constant comparison with others only deepened this suffering. "We must learn to be content with what we have," he said, "and find satisfaction within ourselves rather than seeking it from external sources."

The Stoic philosopher nodded in agreement, adding, "Indeed, true happiness comes from mastering our desires and emotions, not from external circumstances." "We should focus on cultivating inner virtues and resilience, for they are the only things within our control." The room buzzed with nods of approval and murmurs of agreement.

A Buddhist monk, dressed in his simple saffron robe, spoke up next. "In our tradition," he began, "we also teach that desire is the cause of suffering. The Buddha taught that to attain true happiness, we must break free from the cycle of desire and attachment. We can achieve inner peace and tranquility by letting go of our cravings and practicing mindfulness."

The conversation flowed effortlessly as representatives from different religious and philosophical traditions shared their wisdom. A common thread emerged: the understanding that excessive desire and constant comparison with others can corrupt the soul and lead to unhappiness.

A Taoist sage said, "The way of the Tao teaches us to live in harmony with the natural flow of life. When we resist the urge to compare ourselves to others and instead embrace our unique path, we can find balance and happiness in our lives."

A Sufi mystic known for his poetic expressions of divine love added, "True contentment comes from recognizing the divine spark within ourselves and others. When we focus on our connection to the Divine, the allure of material wealth and comparison fades away, and we are left with the joy of spiritual fulfillment."

As the sun began to set, casting a warm golden glow over the gathering, the wise figures marveled at the unity of their teachings. Though their paths were different, their core message was the same: that true happiness lies in transcending the trappings of desire, comparison, and material wealth and instead cultivating inner virtues, mindfulness, and spiritual connection. They parted ways with a shared sense of understanding and camaraderie, each returning to their respective corners of the world to share their wisdom and inspire others to seek a trustworthy source of happiness.

One effective psychological method that can help people refrain from meaningless comparisons, reduce jealousy, and increase gratitude is Cognitive-Behavioral Therapy (CBT). CBT is a well-established, evidence-based psychotherapy that identifies and changes negative thought patterns and behaviors contributing to emotional distress.

The core principle of CBT is that our thoughts, emotions, and behaviors are interconnected, and by changing one aspect of this triad, we can positively impact others. For example, by challenging negative thoughts about oneself or one's circumstances, an individual can alter their emotional state and adopt healthier behaviors.

In the context of reducing comparisons and jealousy and promoting gratitude, CBT can be applied in the following ways:

1. Identifying negative thoughts: The first step is recognizing when you engage in unhelpful comparisons or experience jealousy. For example, you might think, "I wish I had a job like my friend's. They must be so much more successful than me." Another example might be thinking, "Their life seems perfect; I'll never have that." By becoming aware of these thoughts, you can begin to challenge them.

2. Challenging negative thoughts: Once you've identified negative thoughts, ask yourself if they are accurate or based on evidence. In the case of the job comparison, question whether your friend's success solely depends on their job or if other factors contribute to their well-being. Another approach is to consider what other aspects of your life might be fulfilling, even if your job isn't exactly what you desire. In the second example, remind yourself that people often only showcase their best moments on social media, and nobody's life is perfect.

3. Reframing thoughts: Replace negative thoughts with more balanced, realistic ones. Instead of thinking, "I'll never be as successful as my friend with their impressive job," reframe it to, "Success is subjective, and I can define it on my own terms." In another instance, instead of focusing on the perceived perfection of someone's life, remind yourself that everyone faces challenges, and it's important to focus on your journey.

4. Developing gratitude: Cultivate gratitude by focusing on the positive aspects of your life and what you appreciate. Start a daily gratitude journal where you write down three things you are grateful for daily. Additionally, consider sharing your gratitude with others by expressing appreciation for their kindness or support. This practice fosters a sense of gratitude within yourself and helps build stronger relationships with others.

5. Implementing behavioral changes: As you start to shift your thought patterns, take action to reinforce your new mindset. For example, if you frequently compare your life to others on social media, commit to spending less time on those platforms and more time engaging in activities that bring you genuine joy and satisfaction. Additionally, consider volunteering or participating in community events, which can shift your focus from comparisons to

making meaningful connections and contributing positively to others' lives.

6. Evaluating progress: Regularly review your thought patterns, emotions, and behaviors to assess the impact of CBT techniques on your well-being. For instance, after a few weeks of practicing gratitude journaling and reducing social media usage, reflect on whether you feel less envious and more content with your life. It is also helpful to discuss your progress with a trusted friend or mental health professional who can provide support and guidance as you work to develop healthier thought patterns and behaviors.

By consistently practicing these CBT techniques, individuals can develop healthier thought patterns, reduce jealousy and comparisons, and cultivate a more grateful and content mindset.

Comparison can be a significant hindrance to successful financial planning, as it may lead individuals to make decisions based on what others are doing rather than what is best for their financial goals. It's essential to recognize the detrimental impact of comparison and develop strategies to resist the temptation to follow others blindly.

Imagine a scenario where you have carefully crafted a conservative investment portfolio that aligns with your long-term goals and risk tolerance.

You feel confident in your strategy, but then you hear stories of friends or colleagues who have experienced substantial returns this year by investing in riskier assets. The allure of potentially higher gains can be challenging to resist, and you may question your initial strategy.

You might shift your portfolio and invest in those risky assets to match your friends' success. However, this decision does not consider the volatility of such investments, which could lead to significant losses in the future. The risky assets might crash the following year, leaving you with a financial setback that could have been avoided had you stuck to your original plan.

As we traverse the winding path of life, it becomes apparent that comparison, measuring ourselves against others, can be a treacherous and insidious force. Much like the mythical Sirens that lured sailors to their doom with their enchanting voices, comparison whispers seductive tales of what could be, tempting us to stray from the course that is true to our nature.

In our pursuit of happiness and fulfillment, we often become entangled in the web of comparison, losing sight of the unique journey that we are meant to undertake. We become mired in the belief that the grass is always greener on the other side, and in doing so, we fail to appreciate the verdant meadow beneath our feet.

Ancient philosophers and spiritual traditions have long warned against the perils of comparison. From the Stoics, who counseled that we should focus on what is within our control, to the teachings of Buddhism, which emphasize the impermanence of all things and the need to release attachment, these wise sages recognized the futility of seeking happiness in the external world.

To escape the clutches of comparison, we must learn to cultivate gratitude for the abundance in our lives. Gratitude is the balm that soothes the restless soul, reminding us of the countless blessings we have been granted. The compass guides us back to our true selves, where contentment and inner peace reside.

In the words of the poet Rumi, "Be grateful for whatever comes because each has been sent as a guide from beyond." By embracing gratitude, we can learn to navigate the turbulent waters of comparison, charting a course toward serenity and fulfillment.

So let us unshackle ourselves from the chains of comparison and rejoice in the unique beauty that each of our lives holds, for it is only by recognizing and cherishing the gifts that we already possess that we can find true happiness and live a life imbued with meaning and purpose.

Chapter 17: How to Get out of Paycheck to Paycheck

Marcus Thompson's life was a constant struggle to make ends meet. Working two jobs, he barely scraped by, living from paycheck to paycheck. With financial uncertainty bearing down on him, Marcus often felt hopeless and trapped in his circumstances. However, during these trying times, he discovered a burning desire to break free from poverty and build a better future for himself and his family.

In a recent interview with Forbes, Marcus revealed the emotional turmoil he experienced during his days of hardship. He often felt the crushing weight of exhaustion and doubt, questioning whether he could ever rise above his circumstances. However, precisely these moments of despair forged Marcus's unyielding determination to escape the paycheck-to-paycheck cycle.

Marcus's journey was anything but smooth. In the early days of his business, he faced numerous challenges and setbacks. He had to balance his day jobs with the demands of his fledgling business, often working late into the night to fulfill orders and manage the website. Additionally, he faced skepticism from friends and family, who doubted the viability of his venture.

Undeterred by the difficulties, Marcus soldiered on, driven by his relentless determination to create a better life. He knew success would not come overnight but refused to give up. Marcus invested every spare minute into learning and developing the skills needed to grow his business, and this unwavering commitment to self-improvement ultimately paid off.

As his business began to gain traction, Marcus faced new challenges, such as managing inventory, expanding his product line, and maintaining customer satisfaction. Despite the obstacles, he persevered, using each challenge as an opportunity to learn and grow.

Today, Marcus's story is a beacon of hope and inspiration for those trapped in the paycheck-to-paycheck cycle. His journey is a testament to the power of persistence, determination, and self-belief in overcoming life's obstacles and achieving success. Through his hard work, Marcus has built a thriving business and transformed his life and family, proving that anything is possible with grit and determination.

Emily Johnson was no stranger to the struggle of living paycheck to paycheck. As a single mother working multiple jobs, she constantly juggled bills, childcare, and the everyday challenges of raising a family. Emily knew she needed to find a way to break free from her financial struggles and create a better life for her children. Little did she know that her journey would lead her to become a successful entrepreneur and motivational speaker.

Growing up in a low-income household, Emily was always familiar with financial hardships. While raising her two young children, she was determined to give them a life she never had. However, with limited job opportunities and mounting expenses, Emily is stuck in a vicious cycle of debt and despair.

In an interview with Entrepreneur Magazine, Emily shared her emotional journey from living paycheck to paycheck to achieving financial success. She spoke of the countless sleepless nights of worry and anxiety about her family's future. During these difficult times, Emily realized she had to take control of her destiny and make a change.

Drawing from her passion for fitness and health, Emily started her own business as a personal trainer. She began by offering free training sessions to friends and acquaintances, using social media to showcase her client's success stories. As her reputation grew, Emily faced numerous challenges, including finding the time and energy to manage her business alongside her other jobs and overcoming the skepticism of those around her.

Despite the obstacles, Emily remained steadfast in her pursuit of success. She studied business strategies, marketing, and social media management in her spare time, slowly building her client base and expanding her services. Her dedication paid off when a local celebrity, impressed by Emily's determination and results, began to train with her and shared her progress with their followers. This exposure led to a significant increase in clientele, allowing Emily to quit her other jobs and focus solely on her growing business.

Today, Emily's fitness empire has expanded to include online training programs, a successful YouTube channel, and a fitness apparel line. As a motivational speaker, she shares her inspiring story with others struggling financially, empowering them to take control of their lives and overcome adversity.

David Parker's story is one of unwavering determination and resilience. Despite multiple failures, including bankruptcy, he never lost sight of his dream to escape the paycheck-to-paycheck cycle and build a better life. Today, he stands as the CEO of a thriving tech company, an inspiring testament to the power of perseverance in the face of adversity.

Living paycheck to paycheck had become a way of life for David. With mounting debts and an uncertain financial future, he knew that something had to change. In a recent interview with Inc. Magazine, David recounted his journey from financial despair to entrepreneurial success, shedding light on his numerous challenges and setbacks.

Determined to turn his life around, David pursued his passion for technology and started a small software development company. However, his initial venture could have been more challenging. He struggled to find clients, and the few projects he did manage to secure could have generated more income to cover his expenses. To make matters worse, David filed for bankruptcy after a business partnership went sour, leaving him in a dire financial situation.

Undeterred by his failures, David remained steadfast in his pursuit of success. He learned from each setback, refining his business strategy and improving his skills as an entrepreneur. Over the years, he launched several other ventures with varying degrees of success. Although some of these endeavors failed, David refused to relinquish his dream of breaking free from the paycheck-to-paycheck cycle.

As David's knowledge and experience grew, so did his reputation within the tech industry. He began to attract clients from larger, more established companies, and his software development business slowly started to gain traction. Despite facing numerous obstacles, including fierce competition and tight deadlines, David remained committed to his vision and continued to push forward.

It was not until David's innovative software solution caught the attention of a major tech giant that his fortunes finally began to change. Impressed by his product, the company signed a lucrative contract with David, providing the financial stability he had long sought. This breakthrough allowed him to expand his business, hire additional staff, and break free from the paycheck-to-paycheck cycle.

The stories of Marcus Thompson, Emily Johnson, and David Parker offer valuable insights into the journey from financial hardship to success. Despite their different backgrounds and industries, these individuals share common traits and strategies that allowed them to overcome the paycheck-to-paycheck cycle. By examining their experiences through the lens of psychology and success principles, we can distill valuable lessons for those seeking to break free from economic challenges.

1. Persistence: All three stories showcase the importance of persistence. Marcus, Emily, and David each faced numerous setbacks and challenges but remained committed to their goals. Their unwavering determination allowed them to persevere through hardships and ultimately achieve success. This aligns with the widely-accepted success principle of "grit" – the ability to maintain effort and interest over long periods despite failures, setbacks, and plateaus in progress (Duckworth, 2016).

2. Continuous Learning: Each individual is committed to continuous learning, acquiring new skills, and refining their strategies to grow their businesses. This mindset of constant self-improvement is a cornerstone of success literature, with Napoleon Hill's "Think and Grow Rich" (1937) emphasizing the importance of specialized knowledge and lifelong learning.

3. Adaptability: Marcus, Emily, and David all displayed adaptability by pivoting their strategies and adjusting their approach in the face of changing circumstances. This ability to adapt is a key factor in success, as highlighted by Charles Darwin's famous quote: "It is not the strongest of the species that survives, nor the most intelligent; it is the one most responsive to change."

4. Resilience: Resilience, the ability to bounce back from failures and setbacks, is a common thread in all three stories. David, in particular, faced bankruptcy and multiple failed ventures before achieving success. Psychological research has shown that resilience is critical in overcoming adversity and achieving long-term success (Masten, 2001).

5. The Power of Networking and Social Support: Social networking and social support influenced each individual's journey. Marcus and Emily benefited from influential figures sharing their businesses with a broader audience, while David's growing reputation

in the tech industry helped secure lucrative contracts. Social support and networking are essential to success, with psychologist Robert Cialdini's "Influence: The Psychology of Persuasion" (1984) discussing the power of social proof and reciprocity in building credibility and influence.

6. Clear Goal-Setting: A clear vision and well-defined goals are evident in the stories of Marcus, Emily, and David. Each of them had a specific objective – to break free from the paycheck-to-paycheck cycle and build a better life for themselves and their families. This concept aligns with the SMART goal-setting framework (Doran, 1981), which emphasizes creating specific, measurable, achievable, relevant, and time-bound objectives.

Living paycheck to paycheck can significantly affect an individual's mental and emotional well-being. The relentless pressure to make ends meet and the constant stress of financial uncertainty can lead to feelings of depression, anxiety, and hopelessness. However, there is hope for those willing to harness the power of their minds and their determination to break free from this cycle. The narrative below will explore and sum up some of the psychological impacts of financial hardship and offer encouragement for those seeking to use the power of their minds and determination to create positive change in their lives.

The story begins with an individual trapped in the paycheck-to-paycheck cycle, struggling with mounting debts and a seemingly endless string of expenses. This person's life is filled with stress, anxiety, and fear, and the weight of their financial situation is taking its toll on their mental and emotional health.

One day, this individual stumbles upon the teachings of the famous psychologist William James, who believed that human being could alter their life by altering their attitudes of mind. This idea sparks a fire within them, igniting a newfound sense of hope and possibility. They realize that the key to breaking free from the paycheck-to-paycheck cycle lies in their mindset and determination, not external circumstances.

As the individual delves deeper into this newfound understanding, they come across the work of psychologist Carol Dweck and her concept of a growth mindset. They learn that by embracing challenges, persisting in the face of setbacks, and learning from criticism, they can develop the mental resilience needed to overcome the paycheck-to-paycheck cycle. Inspired by this idea, they cultivate a growth mindset and set their sights on a brighter financial future.

Fueled by their new outlook, the individual starts to visualize their ideal life, free from the constraints of living paycheck to paycheck. They create a clear vision of their goals and the steps needed to achieve them, combining this visualization with SMART goal-setting techniques to stay focused, motivated, and committed to their objectives.

Determined to make their vision a reality, the individual starts taking decisive action to improve their financial situation. They seek new personal and professional growth opportunities, such as furthering their education or exploring new career paths. Along the way, they encounter challenges and setbacks but remain steadfast in their commitment to breaking free from the paycheck-to-paycheck cycle.

Recognizing the importance of support and connection, the individual begins to build a network of like-minded individuals who share their goals and aspirations. Together, they exchange ideas, share resources, and find inspiration in the stories of others who have successfully overcome financial hardship. This support network is a constant reminder of the power of determination and the strength of pursuing a common goal.

As individuals continue to act and progress toward their goals, they slowly but surely see improvements in their financial situation. Over time, they break free from the paycheck-to-paycheck cycle and build a life of financial stability and abundance.

The journey of overcoming the struggles of paycheck-to-paycheck living is not easy, but it is possible for those willing to harness the power of their minds and determination. Individuals can rise above their circumstances and build a prosperous future free from financial struggle by cultivating a growth mindset, setting clear goals, and taking decisive action.

Chapter 18: Seeking The Balance

In the small town of Harmony, five friends gathered for their monthly dinner at Sarah Thompson's house. The group consisted of Sarah Thompson, a frugal minimalist; Jake Collins, a wealthy businessman; Emily Robinson, a passionate artist; David Martinez, a dedicated teacher; and Lily Adams, a non-profit director. Over the years, the friends had gone their separate ways, but they remained close and valued their time together.

As the friends sat around Sarah's modest dining table, they discussed their lives, successes, and struggles. Sarah, a content minimalist, expressed her satisfaction with her simple life. She had few possessions and spent her days tending to her garden and volunteering at the local animal shelter. However, she admitted feeling a lack of motivation to pursue anything beyond her current circumstances.

On the other hand, Jake shared his most recent business accomplishments, but he couldn't hide the strain in his voice. His wealth had grown exponentially, but he needed more time for work. His relationships were suffering, and he felt a void his material possessions couldn't fill.

Emily, the artist, listened intently to her friends and offered her perspective. "Money is important, of course, but so is following your passions and nurturing your relationships. I may not have as much as Jake, but I've found balance by pursuing my art and spending quality time with my loved ones."

David, the teacher, agreed with Emily. "I chose a profession that doesn't pay as much as others, but it gives me a sense of purpose. I find satisfaction in helping my students grow and achieve their dreams. I make a point to manage my finances well and still make time for friends and family."

Lily said, "My work with the non-profit has shown me how important it is to live a balanced life. We strive to make a difference in our community and prioritize human connection over material wealth. It's about finding the middle ground between Sarah's minimalism and Jake's pursuit of material success."

As the conversation unfolded, the friends realized the importance of introspection and self-awareness in finding balance. They acknowledged that their paths had strengths and weaknesses, but they all had something valuable to learn from one another.

In the following months, the friends consciously tried to apply the lessons they had learned during that memorable dinner. Sarah began exploring new hobbies and interests, pushing herself to grow and develop. Jake reevaluated his priorities and began dedicating more time to his relationships and personal well-being, even if it meant slowing down his pursuit of wealth.

Emily, David, and Lily continued to prioritize their passions, relationships, and purpose, ensuring their lives remained rich and meaningful. They all found that by embracing a more holistic approach to success, they could enjoy financial stability without sacrificing their happiness and well-being.

In pursuit of a fulfilling life, individuals often traverse the delicate balance between financial freedom and material wealth. This journey may lead them down two paths, each with unique challenges and rewards. Striking for perfect harmony is essential in fostering a sense of well-being and happiness while enjoying financial stability benefits.

The minimalist lifestyle, which emphasizes frugality and values experiences over possessions, has become increasingly popular. Advocates of minimalism discover freedom in living with the bare minimum, finding richness in meaningful connections and moments rather than material belongings. Financial freedom, in this context, signifies the ability to meet basic needs and enjoy life without being constrained by societal expectations or the endless pursuit of material possessions.

However, minimalism can sometimes result in complacency and stagnation, as individuals may need more motivation to improve or grow. The drive to learn and take risks might wane when content with just enough, leading to a diminished sense of purpose and fulfillment.

On the other end of the spectrum, some individuals dedicate themselves to the relentless pursuit of material wealth, often at the expense of personal relationships and overall happiness. While financial success may offer security and accomplishment, this unending chase can lead to dissatisfaction, stress, and meaningless life.

Materialism, too, can be detrimental to one's well-being. Studies have shown that an excessive focus on material possessions correlates with reduced happiness, increased stress, and weakened social connections. Moreover, the constant pursuit of wealth and possessions can generate a never-ending cycle of discontent as individuals continuously seek the next best thing.

Individuals must first understand their motivations and values to harmonize these conflicting approaches. Through introspection, self-awareness, and examining one's priorities, it is possible to identify what truly matters and align actions with those values. In doing so, contentment and purpose can be achieved without sacrificing happiness or relationships.

A balanced approach to success considers factors beyond financial wealth and material possessions. It encompasses nurturing personal relationships, pursuing passions, and cultivating a sense of purpose. By adopting a more holistic perspective on success, individuals can foster a sense of well-being and fulfillment that is not solely dependent on material wealth.

Practical strategies for finding balance include setting realistic financial goals, maintaining a budget, and saving for the future, while simultaneously making time for personal relationships and self-care. Prioritizing experiences and personal growth over material possessions can help create a more satisfying and meaningful life.

The journey to financial freedom often begins with the pursuit of passive income. While it may seem counterintuitive, achieving financial freedom does not equate to a life of idleness. Studies have shown that engaging in meaningful activities is crucial to human well-being and happiness. One such study, conducted by psychologists Kennon M. Sheldon and Tim Kasser, found that individuals who focused on intrinsic goals, such as personal growth and relationships, experienced greater well-being and happiness than those who prioritized extrinsic goals, like wealth and fame.

Financial freedom opens doors to a more meaningful and fulfilling life when viewed as a means rather than an end. No longer shackled by the need to work for money, individuals can redirect their time and energy towards higher-end pursuits, such as personal growth, relationships, and contributing to society. Money, in this context, becomes a powerful tool that enables individuals to delve deeper into their own life's purpose.

The first step towards leading a more philosophical and fulfilling life is self-reflection. With financial freedom secured, individuals can take a step back and reassess their values, passions, and goals. This reflective process allows them to realign their lives with what truly matters, leading to a more profound sense of purpose and satisfaction.

Next, nurturing personal relationships becomes a paramount concern. Financial freedom provides the opportunity to invest time and energy into the connections that matter most, fostering love, support, and companionship. These strong relationships form the foundation for a fulfilling life, contributing to our sense of belonging and happiness.

Moreover, the pursuit of personal growth takes on a new significance. Financially independent individuals can explore their interests, develop new skills, and continue learning. This continuous growth keeps life exciting and engaging, contributing to more extraordinary accomplishments and self-worth.

In addition to personal growth, financial freedom allows individuals to focus on giving back to society. With the luxury of time and resources, they can devote themselves to philanthropy, volunteering, or community-building efforts. By contributing to the greater good, individuals can derive a sense of fulfillment that transcends material wealth.

Lastly, embracing a life of gratitude and mindfulness further enhances the philosophical journey toward a fulfilling life. Acknowledging the privileges and opportunities that financial freedom affords can foster a sense of appreciation and contentment. Cultivating mindfulness enables individuals to fully experience and savor the present moment, bringing a greater sense of happiness and satisfaction.

Below are some great examples of some historical figures who wisely used financial freedom as a great tool to pursue the higher end meaning for their lives and even the entire humanity:

1. Benjamin Franklin was not only one of the Founding Fathers of the United States but also a renowned polymath who made significant contributions to multiple fields, including science, literature, and politics. After achieving financial

freedom through his successful printing business, Franklin focused on intellectual pursuits and public service. Among his many accomplishments, he is famous for his experiments with electricity, which led to the invention of the lightning rod, and for founding the first public library in America. Franklin also played a crucial role in drafting the U.S. Constitution, shaping the nation's early years.

2. Leonardo da Vinci, a legendary Italian polymath, excelled in various fields, including painting, sculpture, architecture, science, and engineering. After achieving financial stability through his work as an artist and engineer for wealthy patrons, such as the Duke of Milan, da Vinci, he devoted his time to exploring various interests. His artistic masterpieces, including the Mona Lisa and The Last Supper, are celebrated worldwide, while his scientific and engineering sketches reveal a visionary mind centuries ahead of its time. Da Vinci's curiosity and ingenuity have impacted art, science, and human understanding.

3. Charles Darwin, the father of the theory of evolution, came from a well-to-do family, which allowed him to focus on his scientific interests without concern for financial stability. Darwin's groundbreaking work, On the Origin of Species, laid the foundation for modern evolutionary theory and forever changed our understanding of the natural

world. His ideas on natural selection and adaptation provided a new framework for studying biology, geology, and other fields. Darwin's relentless pursuit of knowledge and his dedication to scientific inquiry have left an indelible mark on human history.

4. Bertrand Russell, a prominent British philosopher, mathematician, and social critic, came from an aristocratic family, giving him the financial freedom to pursue his intellectual passions. Russell contributed significantly to logic, mathematics, and philosophy and was awarded the Nobel Prize in Literature in 1950. He was an outspoken advocate for social justice and peace, using his influence to campaign against war and nuclear weapons. Russell's extensive work, including the landmark Principia Mathematica, has impacted diverse disciplines and continues to inspire scholars and thinkers today.

In contrast, below are some examples from the opposite side of the spectrum:

1. Howard Hughes, an American businessman, aviator, and film producer, amassed a significant fortune through his various ventures. However, instead of using his wealth to pursue meaningful goals or contribute to society, Hughes became increasingly reclusive and obsessed with his comfort and luxury. His mental health deteriorated, and he spent his final years in isolation, plagued by eccentric behavior and paranoia. Despite his immense wealth,

Hughes's life was marked by unhappiness and a lack of fulfillment.

2. The "King of Pop," Michael Jackson, earned immense wealth and fame throughout his illustrious career. Unfortunately, Jackson struggled with his finances, spending vast sums on luxurious properties, artwork, and other extravagant purchases. His excessive spending and a series of legal battles and personal issues led to severe financial difficulties later in his life. Jackson's story illustrates the potential pitfalls of prioritizing material wealth and luxury over personal well-being and fulfillment.

3. Elizabeth Holmes, the founder of the now-defunct biotech company Theranos, once boasted a net worth of $4.5 billion, making her the youngest self-made female billionaire. However, instead of using her wealth and influence for the greater good, Holmes misled investors and patients about her company's medical testing technology. Ultimately, her deception was uncovered, and her company dissolved, leaving her with a tarnished reputation and legal troubles. Holmes's pursuit of wealth and status at any cost ultimately led to her downfall.

4. Scott Storch, a successful music producer who worked with top artists like Beyoncé and 50 Cent, squandered his multimillion-dollar fortune on a lavish lifestyle filled with luxury cars, extravagant parties, and expensive drugs. His excessive spending

and addiction problems eventually led to bankruptcy and the loss of his career. Storch's story is a cautionary tale about the dangers of prioritizing material wealth and extravagance over personal well-being and meaningful pursuits.

In the grand dance of life, money weaves its way through our days like a shimmering thread, binding us to the world and all its possibilities. The attainment of financial freedom is but a stepping stone. This gateway unfurls before us like a golden tapestry, inviting us to delve into the boundless depths of our potential. When we unlock the secrets of abundance, we find its true value lies not in the glittering trinkets it can bestow, but in the fertile soil, it provides for the blossoming of our deepest aspirations and dreams.

To harness the true power of wealth, we must resist the siren call of superficial desires and fleeting pleasures that threaten to trap us in a tangled web of dissatisfaction and regret. Instead, let us embrace the opportunity to forge our destinies with purpose and passion, using our newfound freedom to scale the lofty heights of self-discovery, forge meaningful connections with our fellow travelers, and leave our indelible mark upon the world, for it is in the pursuit of these noble endeavors that we find our souls enriched. Our spirits are invigorated, transcending the confines of materialism and soaring to the celestial realms of achievement and fulfillment.

May we remember that the greatest treasures that wealth can offer are not the gilded baubles and sumptuous feasts that adorn our tables but the moments of clarity and wisdom that illuminate our minds, the bonds of love and camaraderie that warm our hearts, and the unwavering pursuit of purpose that fuels our inner fire. When we heed the call to greatness that echoes within us all, we rise above the base instincts of our earthly nature and embrace the radiant light of our true potential, etching our names upon the vast canvas of eternity.

Chapter 19: Debts and Consumerism

The heart of capitalism beats with an insatiable desire for growth, continuously driving the gears of consumption to generate wealth and progress. At its core, the capitalist system thrives on constantly stimulating consumer demand, with media playing an indispensable role in fueling the fire of desire.

Every day, the media use various methods to get people to borrow more money and spend without limits. Advertising, for example, is an important tool company uses to make people feel like they need their products immediately. Advertisements use captivating images, persuasive language, and interesting stories to get people to buy more and more stuff, promising happiness and fulfillment with each new purchase.

Consider the example of the automotive industry. Media campaigns often showcase the latest models' advanced features, fueling the desire for constant upgrades. Consumers are enticed by the promise of better performance, luxurious interiors, and cutting-edge technology. The narrative of 'newer is better' becomes ingrained in the public consciousness, driving the need for auto loans and contributing to the ever-expanding economy.

The fashion industry, too, is a prime example of how the capitalist system harnesses the power of media to spur consumption. Seasonal trends are promoted with great fanfare, creating a sense of urgency to keep up with the latest styles. As a result, fast fashion has emerged, with clothing items quickly becoming outdated, only to be replaced by a new wave of must-have garments. This rapid turnover generates profits for the industry and keeps consumers in a perpetual state of desiring more.

Economic growth is often equated to success and prosperity in a capitalist society. It is through the vigorous promotion of consumption that this growth is achieved. The media, acting as an indispensable cog in this grand machine, manipulates the desires and aspirations of the masses, guiding them toward an endless pursuit of material acquisition. The allure of newer, better, and more advanced products captures the collective imagination, driving the insatiable hunger for consumption at capitalism's core.

The United States is renowned for its material wealth and the promise of the American Dream, where success was measured by economic growth and the accumulation of material possessions. Yet, beneath this glittering consumerism facade lay hidden costs that would slowly reveal themselves over time.

Let us explore the work of notable thinkers who have delved into the depths of the American psyche to uncover the roots of consumerism. John Kenneth Galbraith, a wise economist, saw the imbalance in the nation's values. In his tome, "The Affluent Society," he critiqued the American focus on material wealth and consumption, which led to the neglect of public goods and services. Through his astute observations, Galbraith illuminated the cultural foundations of American consumerism.

Juliet B. Schor, another insightful scholar, examined the social and environmental consequences of this nation's love affair with consumption in her paper, "The Social Costs of Private Consumption." Schor found that constantly pursuing material possessions bred a culture of comparison and competition. This insatiable desire for more resulted in increased debt, environmental degradation, and decreased well-being. Schor's work highlighted the broader social costs of the United States' consumption-driven mindset.

In his thought-provoking book "The Culture of Narcissism," Christopher Lasch linked the rise of narcissism in American society to the nation's fixation on materialism. Lasch argued that the relentless pursuit of self-gratification and material wealth had eroded traditional values such as community, empathy, and self-sacrifice. His analysis offered a psychological perspective on the factors driving American consumerism.

As our tale unfolds, we can discern several vital factors shaping the United States' culture of excessive consumerism. First, the omnipresent influence of advertising and media has played a significant role in normalizing consumption. Advertisements often encourage the belief that material possessions equate to happiness and personal fulfillment, perpetuating a constant desire and dissatisfaction culture.

Second, the nation's preoccupation with economic growth as a measure of success has fostered a culture that values material prosperity above all else. This focus has driven citizens to prioritize personal wealth and consumption in pursuing the American Dream.

Finally, the emphasis on individualism and competition in American society has cultivated a culture of social comparison, where material possessions and conspicuous consumption often measure self-worth.

A curious phenomenon has emerged in the United States: despite mounting debts and vigorous consumer spending, happiness levels have declined. This paradox can be traced to the relentless influence of media, which has subtly molded the public's perception of what constitutes a fulfilling life. By examining authentic data and survey results, we can illuminate the impact of this media-driven narrative on the quality of life in contemporary American society.

A study conducted by the Federal Reserve in 2020 revealed that the total household debt in the United States had reached $14.56 trillion. Broken by category, mortgage debts constituted the largest portion at $10.04 trillion, followed by student loans at $1.57 trillion, auto loans at $1.37 trillion, and credit card debts at $0.82 trillion. This data illustrates Americans' increasing financial burden in their quest for material prosperity.

Meanwhile, consumer spending has exhibited consistent growth over the years. According to the U.S. Bureau of Economic Analysis, personal consumption expenditures increased from $12.29 trillion in 2016 to $13.28 trillion in 2019. This trend suggests a robust appetite for consumption, fueled by the media's relentless promotion of new and improved products.

In contrast to rising debts and spending, happiness levels have declined. The 2021 World Happiness Report placed the United States 19th out of 149 countries, a drop from 13th place in 2016. This deterioration in overall happiness suggests that despite their material wealth, Americans are experiencing less life satisfaction.

A 2019 survey conducted by the American Psychological Association found that 72% of Americans felt stressed about money at least some of the time, with 32% reporting that their financial stress had a significant impact on their mental health. This data highlights the detrimental effect of material pursuits on psychological well-being.

In conclusion, the paradox of consumption in the United States – characterized by escalating debts, vigorous spending, and diminishing happiness – is a testament to the power of media-driven narratives in shaping societal values. The media's promotion of material wealth as the key to happiness has led to a decline in overall life satisfaction and psychological well-being.

There are several countries worldwide where citizens enjoy high happiness without succumbing to excessive consumption. These nations have balanced material comforts and emotional well-being, emphasizing the importance of strong social connections, a healthy work-life balance, and deep harmony with nature. Here are four examples of such countries:

1. Finland: Consistently ranking at the top of the World Happiness Report, Finland boasts a robust welfare system and a high standard of living. Finnish people value their connection with nature, spending time outdoors and engaging in hiking, skiing, and

berry-picking activities. This emphasis on nature and simplicity allows the Finnish to maintain a strong sense of happiness and well-being without excessive consumption.

2. Denmark: Known for its concept of 'hygge,' which translates to a feeling of cozy contentment, Denmark is another country where happiness is not derived from material possessions. Danish prioritize spending time with family and friends, creating a sense of community and belonging. By focusing on these relationships and cultivating a comfortable atmosphere, the Danish maintain their happiness without the pressure to consume excessively.

3. Norway: As one of the wealthiest countries in the world, Norway has a strong social safety net and a high standard of living. However, Norwegian people value more than just material wealth. They appreciate their natural surroundings, with outdoor activities like hiking, skiing, and fishing popular pastimes. This connection with nature and the importance of work-life balance contribute to Norway's high happiness levels, despite a less consumption-driven lifestyle.

4. Iceland: With its small population and close-knit communities, Iceland offers strong social support and camaraderie. The country's focus on sustainable living and environmental conservation demonstrates that happiness can be achieved without reliance on excessive consumption. Icelandic people

enjoy the natural beauty of their country and prioritize spending time with loved ones, fostering a sense of happiness and fulfillment beyond material possessions.

These countries exemplify the idea that happiness can be achieved without overemphasizing consumption. By fostering social solid connections, appreciating the beauty of nature, and maintaining a healthy work-life balance, the citizens of these nations lead fulfilling lives without the pressure to acquire material wealth constantly.

As we navigate the complex world of consumerism and debt, we must learn from the cautionary tales of those facing the consequences of excessive borrowing and spending. In the narrative below, we shall explore the stories of two celebrities who, despite their wealth, succumbed to the pitfalls of overconsumption and debt, as well as two nations that suffered financial crises due to their unchecked greed and reliance on borrowed funds.

First, let us consider the tragic tale of Johnny Depp, the acclaimed actor known for his iconic roles in films such as Pirates of the Caribbean and Edward Scissorhands. At the pinnacle of his career, Depp enjoyed immense wealth and success. However, a lifestyle of extravagance and a series of poor financial decisions led to mounting debts and legal disputes, putting his fortune at risk and tarnishing his once-illustrious reputation.

Similarly, the renowned actress Kim Basinger also fell victim to excessive consumption and debt. After achieving great success in Hollywood, Basinger impulsively purchased the town of Braselton, Georgia, for $20 million, intending to transform it into a tourist destination. However, this ambitious venture proved a financial disaster, ultimately leading to Basinger's bankruptcy in 1993.

On a national level, Greece's financial crisis is a stark reminder of the dangers of unchecked borrowing and spending. For years, Greece enjoyed the benefits of low-interest rates and easy access to credit. However, the nation's excessive borrowing and failure to address its structural issues eventually led to a full-blown financial crisis. As a result, Greece was forced to implement harsh austerity measures, causing widespread economic hardship and social unrest.

Another example can be found in Argentina's long financial crisis history, driven by external shocks and internal mismanagement. The most recent crisis in 2018 resulted from unsustainable borrowing, fiscal deficits, and rampant inflation. The Argentinian government was forced to seek financial assistance from the International Monetary Fund, leading to painful austerity measures and deepening economic and social problems.

These personal and national financial ruin stories starkly warn against the dangers of excessive consumption and debt. As individuals and nations alike, we must balance our desires and means, ensuring that we do not jeopardize our financial stability and long-term well-being in pursuit of fleeting material pleasures. Only then can we hope to avoid the perils of excess and build a sustainable, prosperous future for ourselves and future generations.

Certain debts, such as mortgages and car loans, are often necessary and inevitable for many individuals as they strive to build a life for themselves and their families. Managing these debts responsibly while avoiding unnecessary liabilities is key to achieving financial stability and well-being.

It is crucial to differentiate between good debt and bad debt. Good debt can be considered an investment in one's future, such as a mortgage for a home or a loan for education. These types of debt can ultimately contribute to long-term financial growth and stability. Conversely, bad debt often results from impulsive spending on non-essential items or short-term pleasures with little or no long-term value.

We must balance managing our debts and avoiding excessive borrowing to attain financial freedom. Here are a few guiding principles to help maintain this delicate equilibrium:

1. Prioritize paying off high-interest debts: Focus on reducing debts with the highest interest rates, such as credit card balances, to minimize the overall cost of borrowing and free up resources for other financial goals.

2. Develop a realistic repayment plan: Create a feasible and comprehensive plan to repay your debts, considering your income, expenses, and financial goals. Regularly review and adjust your plan to ensure continued progress toward debt reduction and financial freedom.

3. Build an emergency fund: Establish a financial safety net to cover unexpected expenses, which can help prevent the need for additional high-interest debt in times of crisis.

4. Live within your means: Cultivate a lifestyle that balances your desires with your financial resources, avoiding unnecessary expenses and focusing on long-term well-being rather than immediate gratification.

5. Continuously educate yourself on personal finance: Stay informed about financial management strategies, investment opportunities, and current

economic trends to make informed decisions and maximize your financial potential.

By adopting these principles and diligently managing our debts, we can navigate the path to financial freedom with confidence and resilience. In doing so, we empower ourselves to build a more secure and fulfilling future, unburdened by the weight of excessive debt and financial stress.

In a world where consumerism and debt have become the driving forces behind economic growth, it is crucial to remember that these factors, while beneficial on a macro level, can have detrimental effects on individual happiness. As we strive for financial freedom, defined by passive income exceeding our expenses, we must recognize debt's significant role in our financial well-being.

Debt, as a major component of our expenses, can easily overshadow the joys of life, leaving us feeling shackled and burdened. In our quest for personal happiness and financial stability, let us embark on a journey to minimize or, whenever possible, avoid debt altogether.

We must begin by reevaluating our priorities and differentiating our needs and wants. By focusing on meeting our essential needs first and scrutinizing our desires, we can make more informed decisions about our expenditures, reducing reliance on debt. This process requires introspection, discipline, and a commitment to living within our means.

Moreover, let us celebrate the beauty of simplicity and embrace a lifestyle that values experiences over material possessions. This shift in perspective can lead to a greater sense of fulfillment and well-being as we learn to find happiness in the intangible aspects of life. As we foster connections with others, appreciate the beauty of nature, and engage in activities that bring us joy, we can create a more meaningful existence that is not dependent on debt-fueled consumerism.

By consciously choosing to minimize debt in our lives, we are taking a stand against the pervasive influence of consumerism and reclaiming our happiness. In doing so, we empower ourselves to pursue a life of financial freedom and genuine contentment, paving the way toward a brighter, more fulfilling future.

Chapter 20: Everything Is Connected

Everything in life is connected, and our goals and values are no exception. To achieve financial freedom, it is essential to prioritize this objective above the pursuit of material possessions. By placing financial freedom at the top of our list, we can save money as early as possible and capitalize on the power of compounding interest.

The story of Warren Buffett, one of the world's most successful investors, demonstrates the importance of aligning goals and values early in life. Buffett began investing at 11 and steadfastly focused on financial independence throughout his career. By prioritizing wealth accumulation over material possessions, he was able to amass a fortune and become one of the world's wealthiest individuals. Buffett's frugal lifestyle and long-term investment strategy serve as an excellent example of how prioritizing financial freedom can lead to significant success.

Another example is the story of actor Ashton Kutcher, who has managed to build a successful investment portfolio alongside his acting career. Kutcher's investments in technology startups like Uber and Airbnb have significantly contributed to his wealth. His focus on long-term financial stability instead of merely enjoying the perks of fame showcases the importance of prioritizing financial freedom.

In contrast, consider the numerous stories of lottery winners who, despite receiving large windfalls, struggle with managing their newfound wealth and often end up in financial ruin. These examples highlight the significance of cultivating a solid financial foundation and aligning one's values with the goal of financial independence. Even the most substantial sums of money can quickly vanish without the proper mindset and priorities.

The concept of minimalism further illustrates the connection between our goals and values. Minimalists can allocate more resources towards saving and investing by intentionally reducing material possessions and living simpler lives. This approach aligns their lifestyle with the pursuit of financial freedom and allows them to focus on what truly matters. Embracing minimalism can help individuals break the cycle of consumerism and work towards a more secure financial future. A well-known minimalist, Joshua Becker, once said, "Minimalism is the intentional promotion of the things we most value and the removal of anything that distracts us from it." By adopting this mindset, we can make more conscious financial decisions and allocate our resources more effectively, bringing us closer to achieving financial freedom.

Society often glorifies and envies the rich, but it is essential to remember that luck and random odds often play a significant role in wealth accumulation. Instead of idolizing or resenting the wealthy, strive for objectivity in your financial decisions. People tend to believe what they want to believe, but this can be detrimental when it comes to investing.

Consider the cases of celebrities such as Johnny Depp or Nicolas Cage, who faced financial ruin despite their immense success due to poor investment choices and extravagant spending habits. Depp, once one of the highest-paid actors in Hollywood, encountered financial troubles after a series of legal battles and excessive spending on luxury items such as real estate, artwork, and a private island. Cage, another successful actor, experienced a similar downfall, squandering his fortune on extravagant purchases, including multiple castles, luxury cars, and rare artifacts. These examples serve as cautionary tales, emphasizing the importance of financial discipline and prudent decision-making.

On the other hand, some celebrities have amassed significant wealth through hard work, talent, and strategic investments. Oprah Winfrey is a media mogul and philanthropist who overcame a challenging childhood to build a media empire and make a lot of money. Winfrey's ability to leverage her success in the entertainment industry into various business ventures demonstrates the value of diversification and financial acumen.

Another noteworthy example is the story of author J.K. Rowling, who went from living on welfare to becoming a billionaire thanks to the success of the Harry Potter series. Her wealth can be attributed to her perseverance, talent, and a healthy dose of luck when a publisher accepted her manuscript after numerous rejections. Rowling's story reminds us that while luck may play a role in wealth accumulation, hard work and determination are crucial factors.

It is essential to recognize that wealth is not always synonymous with happiness or fulfillment. Wealthy individuals may still struggle with personal issues or face the same challenges as everyone else. The story of the late fashion designer Kate Spade reminds us that wealth cannot shield us from all of life's difficulties.

In his book "Outliers," Malcolm Gladwell argues that success is often a combination of talent, hard work, and fortunate circumstances. This perspective challenges the notion that the wealthy solely deserve our admiration and encourages us to be more discerning in our financial pursuits. By dispelling the myths surrounding wealth and adopting a more objective and informed approach to our financial decisions, we can achieve financial freedom sustainably and responsibly.

It's crucial to remember that you can only win some of the time to achieve financial success. Even the most successful investors, like Warren Buffett, have made mistakes and suffered losses. The key is to learn from these experiences and not be discouraged by failure. True wealth is often invisible, as many self-made millionaires live frugally and don't showcase their wealth through ostentatious appearances.

One notable example is the story of Apple, one of the most valuable companies globally. In the early 2000s, Apple's stock price plummeted as the company struggled to compete with rivals like Microsoft. However, investors who held onto their shares through these challenging times were rewarded when the company introduced innovative products like the iPod and iPhone, leading to exponential growth in its stock value. This example underscores the importance of perseverance and a long-term investment strategy, even during adversity.

Warren Buffett has had his share of investment missteps. In the 1990s, he invested in a British supermarket chain, Tesco, which later faced significant financial issues due to an accounting scandal and increased competition. Despite this loss,

Buffett's overall investment portfolio has continued to thrive, emphasizing that it is optional to win every time to achieve overall success.

Another example is Netflix, which faced significant challenges when transitioning from a DVD rental service to a streaming platform. In 2011, the company's stock price plummeted after a controversial decision to separate its DVD rental and streaming services. However, investors who remained patient and maintained their positions in Netflix have since been rewarded, as the company has grown into a global streaming powerhouse.

Regarding frugal living, self-made millionaire and author Thomas J. Stanley's book, "The Millionaire Next Door," highlights the lifestyles of many wealthy individuals who live modestly and avoid ostentatious displays of wealth. These millionaires prioritize saving and investing over excessive spending on material possessions, allowing them to maintain and grow their wealth over time.

Celebrities like Sarah Jessica Parker and Leonardo DiCaprio also exemplify the concept of living frugally despite their significant wealth. Parker, known for her role in the television series "Sex and the City," has spoken about her commitment to living modestly and teaching her children the value of money. DiCaprio, an Oscar-winning actor, has been spotted driving a modest Toyota Prius despite his ability to afford luxury vehicles.

By examining the financial habits of average individuals who have achieved financial success, we can gain further insights into the importance of consistency and discipline. One example is Ronald Read, a Vermont-based janitor and gas station attendant who accumulated an $8 million fortune by his death. Read managed to amass his wealth by living frugally, saving diligently, and investing in a diversified portfolio of blue-chip stocks. His story highlights that financial success is attainable even for those who don't earn high incomes, as long as they remain committed to their long-term financial goals and practice disciplined money management.

One effective tool for generating passive income and achieving financial freedom is investing in Closed-End Funds (CEFs). CEFs are an investment vehicle that can provide a steady income stream, aiding in the pursuit of financial independence. By incorporating CEFs into your investment strategy, you can diversify your income sources and reduce reliance on a single revenue stream.

CEFs differ from traditional mutual funds and exchange-traded funds (ETFs) in that they issue a fixed number of shares, which are then traded on stock exchanges. This structure allows CEFs to employ various investment strategies and potentially generate higher yields than their open-end counterparts. For example, CEFs can use leverage to boost returns, invest in illiquid assets, or pursue aggressive investment tactics. These unique features can lead to higher dividend yields and provide investors with an attractive source of passive income.

Some well-known CEFs with a history of strong performance include the Eaton Vance Tax-Managed Global Diversified Equity Income Fund (EXG) and the PIMCO Dynamic Credit and Mortgage Income Fund (PCI). These funds have consistently delivered solid returns to their shareholders while maintaining a focus on income generation. By researching and selecting high-performing CEFs, investors can benefit from these funds' advantages.

However, it is crucial to acknowledge the risks associated with investing in CEFs. Due to their unique structure, CEFs can trade at a premium or discount to their net asset value (NAV). Investors must carefully consider these price discrepancies when making investment decisions. Additionally, using leverage by some CEFs can amplify gains and losses, increasing the overall risk associated with these investments. As with any investment vehicle, conducting thorough research and understanding the potential risks and rewards before committing capital is essential.

Closed-End Funds can be a valuable tool for generating passive income and working towards financial independence. By incorporating CEFs into a diversified investment portfolio, investors can take advantage of their unique features and benefit from higher yields. However, it is crucial to understand the risks associated with CEFs and conduct thorough research before investing. With careful planning and consideration, CEFs can effectively build wealth and achieve financial freedom.

Our upbringing and background significantly influence our perspective on wealth and money. These factors shape our investment style and our attitudes toward financial freedom. Acknowledging and understanding these influences can help us adapt our strategies and make more informed financial decisions.

Children who grow up in financially stable households may have different views on money than those from less fortunate backgrounds. For example, individuals who have experienced financial hardships during their upbringing might prioritize financial security and be more conservative in their investment approach. On the other hand, those who grew up in affluent families may be more inclined to take risks in their investments, as they have a safety net to fall back on.

Cultural influences also play a significant role in shaping our financial perspectives. In some cultures, saving and frugality are highly valued, while conspicuous consumption and displays of wealth are more prominent in others. These cultural norms can impact how individuals approach their finances, from saving and investing to their overall financial goals.

The stories of successful investors and entrepreneurs from diverse backgrounds can provide insight into how upbringing influences financial perspectives. For example, Sir Richard Branson, the founder of the Virgin Group, grew up in a middle-class family and faced challenges with dyslexia. Branson's upbringing taught him the value of perseverance and creativity, contributing to his success as an entrepreneur and investor.

In contrast, Warren Buffett, often considered the most successful investor of all time, was raised in a financially stable household. His father was a stockbroker and later a congressman, providing Buffett with early exposure to finance. This background instilled in Buffett the value of long-term investing and the importance of discipline in financial decision-making.

Another example is the story of Howard Schultz, the former CEO of Starbucks. Schultz grew up in a low-income family and experienced financial hardship firsthand. This background fueled his ambition and motivated him to create opportunities for financial security for himself and others. Under Schultz's leadership, Starbucks implemented progressive employee benefits such as health insurance and stock options, reflecting his commitment to providing financial stability for the company's workforce.

Living paycheck-to-paycheck is a precarious and stressful existence. To break free from this cycle, it is essential to prioritize financial freedom and make conscious choices to save, invest, and live frugally. By focusing on financial independence as the ultimate goal, we can escape the endless pursuit of material possessions and embrace a more fulfilling, secure life.

One of the first steps to escaping the paycheck-to-paycheck cycle is establishing a realistic budget that accounts for essential expenses while allocating funds for saving and investing. By closely monitoring spending habits and cutting back on non-essential expenses, individuals can accumulate savings that can be used to create an emergency fund or invest in income-generating assets.

The story of Michelle Schroeder-Gardner, the founder of the personal finance blog Making Sense of Cents, illustrates the power of focusing on financial freedom. Schroeder-Gardner and her husband paid $40,000 of student loan debt in just seven months by living frugally, cutting expenses, and increasing their income through side hustles. Their dedication to financial independence allowed them to break free from debt and create a life centered on their values and priorities.

Another inspiring example is Joe Udo, who escaped the paycheck-to-paycheck cycle by prioritizing saving and investing. Udo, the Retire by 40 blog creator, worked as an engineer but was unsatisfied with his work-life balance. He and his wife committed to living frugally and aggressively saving over 50% of their income, allowing Udo to retire at age 38 and pursue his passions while spending more time with his family.

In addition to saving and investing, it is essential to develop multiple income streams to break the paycheck-to-paycheck cycle. This can be achieved through side hustles, freelance work, or even creating a small business. Having multiple income sources provides a safety net and can accelerate progress toward financial independence.

Education and financial literacy also play a critical role in escaping the paycheck-to-paycheck cycle. By continually learning about personal finance, budgeting, and investment strategies, individuals can make informed decisions and take control of their financial future. Participating in financial workshops, reading books, and seeking advice from financial professionals are all effective ways to increase financial knowledge and confidence.

Lastly, adopting a long-term perspective is crucial to achieving financial freedom. Escaping the paycheck-to-paycheck cycle requires patience, discipline, and a commitment to incremental progress. By staying focused on financial independence, individuals can maintain the motivation and resilience to overcome financial obstacles and build a secure future.

In conclusion, the journey toward financial freedom is a complex and interconnected process that requires dedication, discipline, and a willingness to adapt our perspectives and behaviors. By prioritizing financial freedom, learning from our failures, and utilizing effective investment tools like CEFs, we can break free from the constraints of materialism and the paycheck-to-paycheck cycle, ultimately achieving a more prosperous and fulfilling life.

Made in the USA
Las Vegas, NV
18 June 2023